MIKE DARLOW'S WOODTURNING SERIES

Useful Woodturning Projects

FOX CHAPEL
PUBLISHING

©2021 by Mike Darlow and Fox Chapel Publishing Company, Inc., 903 Square Street, Mount Joy, PA 17552.

Useful Woodturning Projects is an original work, first published in 2021 by Fox Chapel Publishing Company, Inc. All rights reserved. No part of this publication may be reproduced, stored in a retrieval system or transmitted, in any form or by any means, electronic, mechanical, photocopying, recording or otherwise, without the prior written permission of the copyright holders.

ISBN 978-1-4971-0157-9

The Cataloging-in-Publication Data is on file with the Library of Congress.

To learn more about the other great books from Fox Chapel Publishing, or to find a retailer near you, call toll-free 800-457-9112 or visit us at *www.FoxChapelPublishing.com*.

We are always looking for talented authors. To submit an idea, please send a brief inquiry to acquisitions@ foxchapelpublishing.com.

Printed in Singapore
First printing

CONTENTS

ACKNOWLEDGEMENTS

Since the publication in 2004 of my previous book, *Turned Chessmen,* I have continued to have about eight woodturning magazine articles published each year. Most have have been published in *The Australian Woodworker* published by Skills Publishing, and in GMC's *Woodturning.* I thank Art, Greg and Steven Burrows at Skills, and Mark Baker at GMC for their support and friendship over many years.

Content from *The Australian Woodworker* is included in chapters 5, 6, 7. 11 and 16. Content from *Woodturning* is included in chapters 1 (Whither Woodturning article , 5, 6 and 13. I apologize for any omissions or inaccuracies in these two statements.

I thank Emily Darlow for posing for the figure 3.3 photograph. Also my wife, Aliki, for her tolerance and editing.

OTHER MIKE DARLOW WOODTURNING PUBLICATIONS

Books

The Practice of Woodturning

The Fundamentals of Woodturning

Bassiswisen Drechseln

Woodturning Methods

Woodturning Techniques

Woodturning Design

DVDs

The Practice of Woodturning

Sharpening Woodturning Tools

The Taming of the Skew

Key

Outlines	————————————————
Hidden detail	— — — — — — — — — — —
Pointing and dimensioning arrows	————————————→
Movement arrows	————————————⟫
Force arrows	————————————▶
Cutting arrows	————————————▷
Center lines and axes	—·—··—·—··—·—··—·—·

	Elevation	Section
Pencil gauge boards	☐	
Backgrounds	☐	
Wood	☐	☐
"	☐	☐
" "	☐	☐
Tool steel	☐	☐
"	☐	☐
Steel ground away		☐
"		☐
Other metals	☐	☐
Cuts		☐
"		☐
"		☐
"		☐
"		☐
"		☐

Chapter 1

INTRODUCTION

My objectives with this book are to revive the turning of useful items, and to inspire readers to seek other useful turning subjects.

In the first four books of my woodturning series I covered the techniques of hand woodturning. The fifth book in the series, *Turned Chessmen* published in 2004, was my first project book. It was forecast to flop by a woodwork book marketing expert. 16 years after publication it continues to sell well. Feedback from buyers confirms that the book's background and history content have been a major factor in the book's success, being appreciated both by the turners, and, when passed on, by the users of those chess sets. This second project book continues that approach, and will thus, I hope, interest even those readers who aren't about to undertake any of its projects.

Instead of focussing on one type of useful turning, this book's projects cover a wide range. Some might consider that range too esoteric. My excuses are that it mirrors my own interests in turning, and illustrates the scope to explore.

The interest in turning useful projects has waned in recent decades. I believe that if turners increase the proportion of useful items in their output they would:

- enjoy their turning at least as much
- gain the potential to enjoy using the turnings they keep
- find that their turnings were better appreciated by others.

By *useful* I mean "can be used for other than aesthetic, contemplative or emotion-creating purposes". A useful turning's usefulness may be entirely due to the turning, as in a pastry-cook's rolling pin. At the other extreme the turning may only add three-dimensional ornament to an item which is no less useful without the turning. Of course useful turnings aren't always bought to be used—most buyers of Japanese tea caddies, such as those in figure 1.1, now buy them as ornaments and souvenirs and continue to make their tea with tea bags.

How to describe turnings which aren't useful in the way I've described? My dictionary of antonyms offers *useless* as the antonym of *useful*. However, aesthetic, contemplative and emotion-creating purposes are valid and certainly not useless. For want of a better term, I shall therefore describe turnings which aren't useful as *non-useful*.

Many now live in surroundings in which the only relatively unaltered natural substances are the air and the tap water. Wood is an obsolescent (becoming obsolete) material, and therefore woodturning is an obsolescent skill. But, if you're reading this, you've probably already decided to disregard this truth and continue enjoy using a lathe to shape wood.

Figure 1.1 Three Japanese-style tea caddies turned from European ash (*Fraxinus excelsior*). They have incurved flanges so that the finely powdered green tea doesn't billow into the air when the lid is lifted, not tugged, off. The top of the lid is almost flat, and during the tea ceremony a bamboo teaspoon or *chashaku* rests on it. In the bottom is a recess to grip on the hand.

The Japanese words for tea caddy are *chaire* and *chaki*. This type is a *natsume*, and is used to store the powdered tea for making thin tea.

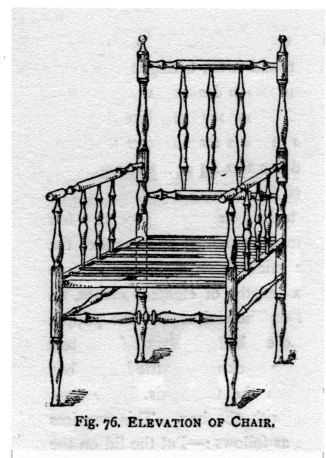

Fig. 76. ELEVATION OF CHAIR.

Figure 1.2 A chair with at least eight designs of identical spindle.

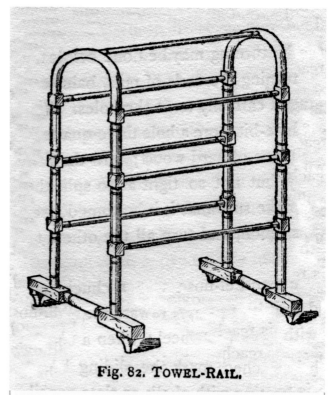

Fig. 82. TOWEL-RAIL.

Figure 1.3 A towel rail constructed from five designs of identical turning.

I contend that during recent decades the hand turning of useful items has declined relative to that of non-useful items. As evidence I cite the 1921 edition of Paul Nooncree Hasluck's *The Wood Turner's Handybook*.[1] Every turning pictured in it is useful as figures 1.2 and 1.3 demonstrate. In contrast, today's woodturning often features non-useful bowls and vessels and the non-turning techniques which are used to apply two-dimensional decoration and three-dimensional ornament.

It's true that during the last 50 years woodturning as an artisan and industrial technique to produce useful items (mainly components for buildings, furniture and woodware) has declined, but not disappeared. It's also true that during that time hobby woodturning has increased in popularity, and it's undoubtedly true that part of that increase is because woodturning has been increasingly promoted as a technique which can be exploited to create Fine Art. In many examples though the turning is a subsidiary technique used to provide a base for the decoration and ornament.

I fully support this widening of woodturning's horizons and ambitions, but not the associated:

- neglect of the potential for useful turnings to be rewarding turning subjects
- narrowing of the range of turning skills which turning teachers offer to beginners and which beginners seek to acquire, and which has thus resulted in a smaller proportion of turners being able to turn useful items
- neglect of pre-turning design.

In this first chapter I'll discuss these changes by considering:

- why the growth in non-useful turning has occurred
- why, in parallel, turning of useful items has declined

This chapter then concludes with some housekeeping matters.

1.1 THE GROWTH IN NON-USEFUL TURNING

I'll discuss the reasons for the growth in non-useful turning under four headings:

- the market for non-useful turnings
- the influence of the woodturning media
- today's high-profile turners
- the influence of turners' associations.

1.1.1 The market for non-useful woodturnings

Michael Dunbar made this insightful statement in his 2016 book *Woodturning Techniques*:[2]

> Modern turners no longer work as subcontractors providing their products to other crafts. Instead, they largely focus on making complete turned objects that stand alone, such as bowls, vases, and platters. . . . Old-time turned objects were inexpensive. . . . Most of the objects made by today's turners are very expensive, selling for prices that will make the uninitiated gasp with disbelief.

Dunbar's statement's first line "modern turners no longer work as subcontractors" suggests that his statement concerns professional woodturners. My assumption from the remainder of the statement is that these turners generate large incomes through producing non-useful one-offs. But is this assumption entirely correct?:

- A proportion of "professional" turners have significant non-turning income. A substantial proportion of some turners' turning incomes comes from demonstrating, teaching, producing paper- and screen-based content about their pieces and techniques, supplying turners, and promoting turning events.
- Some turners' pieces develop and exploit particular techniques or design features. A proportion of these turners earn income by teaching others how to replicate those same techniques or features. Doesn't this suggest that the income from the sales of the originators' pieces may be somewhat fickle?

- There are still some turners, albeit a small number, who earn their entire turning incomes as subcontract (jobbing) turners.
- We only hear of the big-money sales, not about the pieces which don't sell and subsequently clutter their turners' homes.

The last part of Dunbar's statement "the objects made by today's turners are very expensive, selling for prices that will make the uninitiated gasp with disbelief" suggests that those objects aren't priced according to their cost of production, but are priced as if they were Fine Art. The separation of art into high-status Fine Art and lower status craft occurred in Europe during the 18th century. This is not the place to debate the validity of this separation despite its continuing influence, or whether it has been undermined by the subsequent expansion of Fine Art to include such as photography and jazz. But, even if the Fine Art market were as strong as Dunbar implies, can it continue to absorb at worthwhile prices the volume of non-useful turnings being produced?

A factor limiting the acceptance of woodturning as a technique which can be used to create Fine Art is that it uses a lathe, a machine whose raison d'etre is to produce round items quickly. These associations conflict with the widely assumed properties of Fine Art.

1.1.2 The influence of the media

An early catalyst to the growth in non-useful turning was the publication of Dale Nish's book *Artistic Woodturning* in 1980.[3] Its gallery section promoted the non-useful works of several turners. The success of these and other high-profile turners of the non-useful has been and remains a powerful encouragement to the growth in non-useful turning. But, as with the corporate need to build a brand, all professional artists know the importance of building a name. They know that some high prices are due to buyers believing that owning a piece by a name artist bestows status on the buyer, and makes it more likely that the piece will appreciate rather than fall in monetary value over time.

Fortunately the woodturning media rightly believes that in the 21st century it needs bling. Non-useful turnings and the associated techniques, equipment and personalities can provide that bling and much of the content needed by the media of a practice which has an almost static technology. Therefore professional turners of the non-useful have sensibly cooperated with the woodturning media to their mutual benefit. By doing so these turners promote themselves, sales of their pieces, and are more likely to attract teaching and demonstration income.

An unfortunate recent trend is to promote woodturning as fun. This undervalues woodturning which is really about learning, applying that learning, exploration, achievement and modest pride, even though these are sometimes accompanied by frustration and failure. Woodturning also offers opportunities for social interaction.

1.1.3   Today's high-profile turners

Professional turners used to be working class; many had been apprenticed. Today some are tertiary educated, and/or are semi- or fully-retired and comfortably off. These turners may understandably be reluctant to work as jobbing turners once did, producing batches of useful turned building and furniture components and woodware, often designed by others, to order. Instead they're more likely to promote themselves as artists who seek to turn what they conceive. Hobby turners are understandably attracted by this possibility.

1.1.4   The influence of woodturners' associations

Professional turners of the non-useful have been and are hard-working and influential in woodturners' clubs and regional and national associations. Not surprisingly this has and continues to influence the focus of those organisations and the types of turnings their members produce.

The memberships of the British and the American Woodturners Associations are in 2019 about 3,000 plus and 18,000 respectively. These totals are a credit to all past and present officers, although equivalent to only 1 in about 20,000 of their country's populations. Had these

two organisations focussed less on non-useful turning would those numbers be higher? It's impossible to know.

1.2   THE RELATIVE DECLINE IN USEFUL TURNING

The relative decline in useful turning is in part a reaction to the factors discussed in the preceding section, but there are other factors which are discussed below:

* the influence of modernism
* the influence of suppliers
* the misbelief that the range of useful turnings is small
* wood supply and properties
* useful turning is perceived as less creative
* woodturning skills
* design
* demand.

1.2.1   The influence of today's dominant design style

Today's dominant design styles outside woodturning are variants of modernism, a style a century old and defined by Jonathan Woodham as "a 'machine age' aesthetic truly redolent of the twentieth century which, freed from the shackles of historicism, explored new forms and materials that were felt to be symbolically, if not actually, compatible with the mass production capacity of a progressive industrial culture".[4]

Modernism's now not-so-new aesthetic and its rejection of the "shackles of historicism" would if accepted by woodturners largely restrict woodturning's role to producing a small number of turnings whose forms were composed of cylinders, cones and spheres. These are demanding, but boring, to turn by hand. Modernism has also been misinterpreted as a means to ruthlessly minimise cost by applying modern materials and techniques and by stripping away all decoration and ornament. Figures 1.4 to 1.6 illustrate this loss of delightful detailing.

Figure 1.4   A late 19th-century cottage rich in delightful detailing in Goldsmith Street, Goulburn, New South Wales.

Figure 1.6   A 2020 version of a colonial cottage without any delightful detailing. The veranda posts are left-square, there aren't any pilarettes, the barge boards are narrow, and there isn't a finial on the gable end where the barge boards meet.

Figure 1.5   Another view of the cottage shown in figure 1.4. Notice the turned veranda posts, gable finial, pilarettes, drop finials and patera. Alas the finial fixed on top of the gate post is recent and crudely designed, and the tops of the pickets aren't turned, but moulded.

1.2.2   The influence of suppliers

Woodturning suppliers sensibly aim to keep selling to us, and in increasingly-greater volumes. One proven way is to promote new equipment which makes turning easier, an objective which I fully support.

A recent example of such new equipment is the sets of carbide-tipped scrapers introduced in about 2015. These tools do allow you to turn without having to suffer "the drudgery of sharpening" or having to spend a few tens of hours to achieve competence in the conventional techniques. What the advertising for these tools omits is that their use restricts a turner's vocabulary of forms, lengthens the time to turn a design, and also requires more sanding. These disadvantages are however less significant to bowl and vessel turners than turners of useful items which are often spindles or incorporate them. Therefore promoting these tools must have favored a relative expansion in non-useful turning.

1.2.3   The misbelief that the range of useful turnings is small

Some turners complain that the range of useful turnings is very limited. This book's projects may partially dispel that belief, but represent only the tip of a very large iceberg. There are many other sources of ideas for useful turnings if you're prepared to search. Figure 1.7 illustrates just one source—the criticism that some of the uses listed are obsolete is valid, but not necessarily critical.

1.2.4   Wood supply and properties

Wood is becoming relatively more expensive, and the range of available species is declining as is the supply of the straight-grained wood preferred for many useful turnings. In contrast, bowls and vessels can be produced from no- and low-cost found wood.

The decline in professional turning is in part because wood was earlier the only feasible material able to fulfill particular uses. Now these and other uses can be satisfied more cheaply by using materials which do not occur in nature, notably plastic. These substitute materials can also be more practical: wood doesn't fare well in dishwashers.

1.2.5   Useful turning is perceived as less creative and of lower status

By the early 19th century artists and their patrons had persuaded society that art really consisted of the Fine Arts which stimulated an emotional response and even edified behavior, and craft which had more mundane ambitions and consequences. This concept remains powerful today. Hence David Regester's rueful comment: "the idea that the spindle turner [typically a producer of useful turnings] is an inferior beast to the bowl turner [a supposed creator of Fine Art]".[5] Not surprisingly, fewer aspire to be an "inferior beast".

1.2.6   Woodturning skills

Another statement from Michael Dunbar:[2]

> Modern turning also differs from old-time turning in that turners no longer make large numbers of the same object. In other words they do not do a lot of duplication.

Exact duplication is undesirable if you're a turner of Fine Art, but there are two largely-true beliefs which discourage some from attempting useful turning:

- It can require some of the equipment and skills used in cabinetmaking and/or joinery. (Fortunately the growth in woodturning clubs and other communal woodworking facilities including Mens Sheds and SheSheds has improved access to these for turners who don't have the necessary other woodworking equipment themselves.)
- It requires a greater range of turning competence than does non-useful turning.

Is it difficult to achieve competence in the conventional turning techniques? Dale Nish in his book *Creative Woodturning* seems to think so because he states that the cutting method "can be learned only with much practice and patience on the part of the learner. . . The personal satisfaction and sense of achievement derived from a mastering of the cutting method is enjoyed by only a few master woodturners. This goal is something the beginner might set for himself."[3]

But go back in time, and you'll find that turning was regarded as a low-status, low skill trade: "The turning lathe was, and still is, despised as unworthy of a skilled worker".[6] This statement by Gustav Ecke is too damning, but it is true that hand woodturning is not among the most difficult of hand skills. It does not require the high innate artistry of figurative woodcarving, nor the cabinetmakers' ability to use a large range of machines and hand tools to achieve snug fits. Therefore I believe that Nish exaggerates the difficulty of achieving the level of turning competence required for success in useful turning.

How long does it take to acquire a basic range of turning skills? If you don't have any bad turning habits to unlearn and the teaching is sound, in my experience it's about 20 hours of tuition and 20 hours of disciplined practice. Obviously, improvement will continue thereafter, but that 40 hours should provide a sound foundation on which to build greater speed and sureness. Alas, only a minority seem to be prepared to make that commitment. It is true that for many turning is a pastime or a social activity, but should that preclude the initial com-

TABULAR VIEW

OF WORKS IN PLAIN TURNING IN WOOD AND IVORY.

DINING ROOM AND DOMESTIC.

Apple scoops.
Ash trays.

Bellows boards.
Bonbon boxes.
Bottle cases.
Bottle label rings.
Bottle stands.
Bowls.
Bread plates.
Brush handles.
Butter moulds.
Butter stands.

Candle dumps.
Chimney candlesticks.
Candle elevator stands.

Drinking cups.
Dumb waiters.

Egg cups and stands.
Egg glasses.
Epergnes.

Finger plates.

Hand candlesticks.
Hat pegs.

Knife rests.
Knobs for doors, drawers.
  windows. and sticks.

Lamp stands.
Lemon squeezers.
Liqueur frames.

Menu-holders.
Mustard pots.

Napkin rings.
Nightlight stands.
Nut crackers.
Nutmeg graters.

Pepper boxes.
Pickle stands.
Punch bowls.

Rolling pins.

Salad bowls.
Salt cellars.
Sodawater stands.
Spice boxes.
Spill holders.
Snuff boxes.
Stoppers for bottles.
String boxes.
Sugar sifters.

Tables.
Table candlesticks.
Table ware.
Tea caddys.

DRAWING ROOM.

Banner screens.
Bases for glass shades.

Candelabra.
Candle screens.
Card baskets.
Card racks.
Card trays.
Carte de visite frames.
  ditto   on stands.
Chalices.
Chandeliers.
China bowl stands.
Clock cases.
Cocoa nut vases.
Coquilla nut vases.
Cups.

Egg shells as vases.
Etagères.

Flower holders.
Flower pot stands.

Hanging lamp holders.

Jardinières.

Miniature frames.

Ostrich egg vases.

Pagodas.
Pedestals.
Pedestals for bronzes.
Piano candlesticks.
Picture frames.
Pot-pourri jars.

Slender ornaments.
Standard lamp stands.
Stands for China cups.
  ditto   for plates.

Table mirrors.
Tazzas.
Temples.

Vases.

Wall brackets.
Wall light brackets.
Wall mirrors.
Watch stands.
Wax taper stands.
What-nots.

SMOKING ROOM.

Amber mouthpieces.
Ash trays.
Cigar cases.
Cigar cutters.
Cigar stands.
Cigar tubes.
Cigarette cases.
Cigarette moulds.
Horn and ivory mouth-
  pieces.

Pipe bowls.
Pipe stems.
Pipe racks.
Pipe stands.

Spill pots.

Table lights.
Tobacco boxes.
Tobacco jars.

WORK TABLE.

Bodkins and cases.

Crochet needles.

Embroidery frames.
Emery cushions.

Knitting ball holders.

Linen markers.

Needle cases.
Netting meshes.
Netting needles.
Netting vices.

Pin cushions.
Purse moulds.

Reels.
Reel stands.

Screw pincushion work
  holders.
Silk winding machines.
Spinning wheels.
Stilettos.

Tambour frames.
Tatting needles.
Tape measures.
Thimbles.
Thimble cases.

Wax holders.
Winders.
Work cases.
Work boxes.
Worsted ball cases.

Figure 1.7 A list of items to turn published in 1881. Many of the uses are no longer relevant, but new items have since been invented; for example the CD and DVD markers in chapter 10.

TABULAR VIEW
OF WORKS IN PLAIN TURNING IN WOOD AND IVORY.

TOILET.
—

Bonbon boxes.
Bonnet stands.
Bracelets.
Brooches.
Bouquet holders.
Bottle cases.
Buttons.

Chains.
Chatelaines.
Crosses.

Earrings.

Fans.
Folding screens.

Glove stretchers.

Hair rollers.
Hand mirrors.

Jewel cases.

Lipsalve boxes.
Lockets.

Match boxes.
Mirror frames.

Necklaces.

Parasol handles.
Pincushions.
Pin trays.
Pocket mirrors.
Portable hanging wardrobes.
Powder boxes.

Ring holders.

Scarf pins.
Scarf rings.
Scent bottle stands.
Scent boxes.
Shaving brushes.
Shirt studs.
Sleeve links.
Solitaire studs.
Sovereign boxes.

STUDY AND SCIENTIFIC.
—

Almanacks.

Barometers.
Brush penwipers.

Compass cases.

Electrical apparatus.
Erasers.

Hygrometers.

India rubber holders.
Inkstands.

Letter balances.
Letter holders.

Magnifier frames.
Microscope stands.

Opera glasses.

Paper weights.
Pedestal for globes.
Pencil cases.
Penholders.
Penracks and cases.

Rulers.

Seal handles.
Sundials.

Taper stands.
Telephones.
Telescopes.
Telescopes, cases and stands.
Thermometers.

GAMES AND TOYS.
—

Bandelores.
Bagatelle balls.
Besique markers.
Billiard balls.
Billiard chalk cases.
Bowls.

Chessmen.
Cone to run up hill.
Conjuring tricks.
Cribbage boards and pegs.
Croquet balls.
Croquet mallets.
Cup and ball.

Dice.
Dice boxes.
Draughtsmen.

Hoop sticks.
Humming tops.

Military tactics.

Ninepins.

Pegtops.
Pope Joan Boards.
Portable Chessmen.
Puzzles.

Rattles.
Solitaire boards.
Spinning tops.

Toy, breakfast, dinner, dessert, and tea services.

Whipping tops.
Whist counters.
Whist markers.

MISCELLANEOUS.
—

Acoustic instruments.

Bells of speaking tubes.

Castanettes.
Chairman's hammers.
Chinese balls.
Crutches.

Geometrical solids.
Gum rings.

Handles for carpenter's tools.
Handles for turning tools.
Harness rings.
Horse cradles.

Mallets.
Mauls.
Measures.
Musical instruments.
   ,, clarionettes.
   ,, drumsticks.
   ,, flageolettes.
   ,, flutes.
   ,, piccolos.
   ,, oboes and others.
   ,, violin pegs.

Pestles and mortars.
Profile rings.

Solids in ball.
Solid profiles.
Star in ball.

Turned furniture.

Voice conductors.
Violin string boxes.

Walking sticks.
Watch rattles.
Weights.
Whip handles.
Whip racks.
Whistles.

Figure 1.7 continued The list is scanned from: Holtzapffel, John Jacob. *Hand or Simple Turning.* New York: Dover Publications, 1976, pp. 458 and 459. (Originally published in 1881.)

mitment of a mere 40 hours for a hobby which might be pursued for decades? Perhaps because the true situation isn't explained to them, beginners mistakenly believe that all-round turning competence is beyond them.

Malcolm Gladwell in the second chapter of his popular 2008 book *Outliers* opined that to fulfill a person's potential for demanding activities such as computer programing, violin playing to concern standard, lawyering, etc. needs about 10,000 hours of practicing, equivalent to 5 year's full-time.[7] Woodturning is a far less demanding activity, and therefore much less than 10,000 hours is needed for the enthusiastic amateur to achieve competence.

Two factors which Gladwell doesn't properly cover are:

- The asymptotic nature of acquiring skill through instruction and practice. (An *asymptote* is a 'straight line which is approached more and more closely by a curve, but not met by it.) As figure 1.8 illustrates, acceptable competence can be achieved in only a small proportion of the time needed for mastery.
- Learning and practicing inferior rather than optimal techniques ensures that only partial competence can be achieved. To later achieve high competence would require ingrained suboptimal techniques to

be "unlearned" before the optimal techniques could be learned.

Tuition

Woodturning involves manipulating a sharp edge and usually an adjacent bevel against wood moving at high velocity. Turning is peculiar that the risk of a catch can only be reduced by increasing one's turning competence, not by taking more but thinner cuts. And a person's turning competence is strongly related to the quality of the techniques learnt and to the commitment to continue to replicate them.

Teachers typically teach the techniques which they themselves use. These techniques may not be optimal. I doubt that there is an international consensus on which techniques are optimal and their exact details. Further, there is a reluctance to objectively compare the conflicting techniques promoted by different turning teachers.

There may also be a shortage of sound tuition in the full range of basic turning techniques. Much of the tuition advertised is focussed on turning bowls and vessels. It follows that those who thus achieve competence in the limited range of turning techniques usually associated with bowl and vessel turning will tend to avoid attempting designs which require competence in other turning techniques. If there is to be a resurgence in turning useful objects, there has to an increase in the range of techniques taught by turning teachers.

Paul Krugman, Nobel Prize-winning economist and a columnist for the *New York Times,* in 2003 exposed a similar situation to that of woodturning teaching when writing about of all subjects English food: "a free-market economy can get trapped for an extended period in a bad equilibrium in which good things are not demanded because they have never been supplied, and are not supplied because not enough people demand them".[8]

A related problem is that a considerable proportion of beginners don't seek formal tuition. Instead they're self-taught and/or are taught inferior techniques by a well-meaning person. This of course lessens the demand for, and therefore the supply of, quality teaching of the full range of turning techniques.

I have recently taught a class of typical amateurs: in their 50s and 60s, been turning for several years, sold a

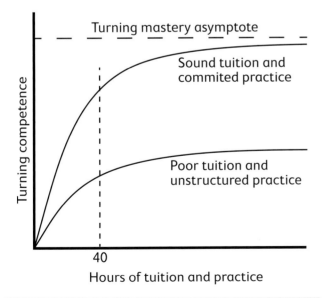

Figure 1.8   The asymptotic nature of acquiring woodturning expertise.

few turnings at markets, and in my opinion with little idea of how to perform even the basic cuts surely and efficiently. But by focussing on turning one-offs, avoiding difficult cuts, and using excessive sanding they were able to produce turnings which were admired. Their reaction to the tuition was revelatory: new potential opened up, confidence was gained. However this was accompanied by the realisation that most of their earlier turning experience had been a waste.

1.2.7   Design

You should design *before* you turn. To many turners design is an alien and onerous practice. They therefore favor non-useful turning in which informal designing *as* you turn is common even though wood which has been undesirably cut away can't be restored to its former state.

Design is the important input—the turning should be the easy part you do at the end. But if your turning technique is poor, you'll tend to neglect designing—why bother with it when you're unlikely to be able to turn what you might design? However once you are a competent turner, the quality of your design greatly influences the quality of your turning output. For example the new gate-post finial in the foreground of figure 1.5 has been competently turned (on an automatic lathe), but is of uninspired design.

A misconception which favors the non-useful is that designing useful turnings is less creative than designing non-useful. Useful-turning design can be more demanding because it is constrained by the need to satisfy use in addition to other objectives. And usefulness is not incompatible with design excellence or beauty.

It's true that many hand turners like to produce ornament. I absolutely agree that the ornament of many of this book's projects is historic in style. But once a design, a style or a design feature is invented, it instantly becomes historical. Is it important whether the invention occurred a day, a year, a century, or a millennium ago? Many of the notable wooden bowls and vessels turned in recent decades have forms resembling examples produced in antiquity in other materials, but this doesn't seem to be regarded adversely.

The reality of design

It's sad but true that we aren't all created equal. Most of us don't have the high innate artistry needed to design pieces of conspicuous originality and merit. Thus artifice and plagiarism are a feature of some non-useful turnings. In contrast, a useful turning may resemble earlier examples, may have to if usefulness is to be retained, but because it is not attempting to be original, accusations of plagiarism are much less likely, relevant or important.

Even copying, unless absolute exactness is specified, can be an exciting design challenge. A tweak here, a millimeter there, can transform a stolid design into one which has life.

1.2.8   The demand for useful turnings

An important factor which I have so far ignored is that the potential demand for useful turnings is far greater than that for non-useful, and could be better exploited.

For most turners sales are of no or little importance; they keep their turnings or give them away. My experience is that most recipients of free turnings would prefer that they were useful. And even if that use is nominal or obscure, it adds an extra dimension of interest.

Look around the homes of non-turners and compare the number of useful turnings with the number of non-useful. I venture that you'll usually find that the former is considerably greater. It's true that the market for useful turnings has declined, in part because of the substitution of man-made materials for wood and the replacement of hand turning by cheaper processes. Therefore a hand-turned item is now a luxury object irrespective of whether it's useful or not, and its design and making should complement that reality.

Many live and/or work in buildings bereft of aesthetic merit whose rooms before furnishing have all the visual interest of the inside of a cardboard box. Hence the desire to compensate by furnishing with posters, pictures, ornaments, etc. This creates an opportunity for woodturners. A useful turning, even something as mundane as chapter 3's backscratcher, can become an object of comfort and affection.

1.3 CONCLUSION

My contention that turners would benefit from increasing their proportion of useful output is against the trend, but is it ill-founded? If you're an amateur turner, you should treat turning how you want to. If you want to treat it as an occasional pastime, that's fine. But to gain real enjoyment you'll need to commit. That doesn't preclude you turning what you want to: it facilitates it. But, as I hope the above has shown, that choice has likely been influenced by factors that you may not have been conscious of. I hope that this book will tempt you to consider increasing your useful output and, if necessary, increasing the range and depth of your turning skills and your interest in design.

1.4 GENERAL MATTERS

This book assumes that you're familiar with the basic woodturning techniques. It therefore repeats little content from my earlier woodturning books, but does explain techniques which are out of the ordinary and particular to a project. I have provided dimensioned scale drawings of the projects, usually in the form of pencil gauges. I don't claim copyright on any of my designs for this book. You're therefore free to copy, modify, or scale them. If you do, it wouldn't belittle you to mention the source.

Many readers will, like me, have drills with imperial and metric diameters. However for woodturners millimeters are a far more convenient unit of measurement than inches. Therefore unless it's appropriate to use a drill with an imperial diameter, I'll usually dimension drill and hole diameters in millimeters, and you can instead choose to use a drill with a close imperial diameter. Note that a greater range of drill diameters are available from specialist engineering suppliers than from most hardware shops. I've also assumed that axial holes in turnings will be bored in the lathe.

The range of possible chucks and chucking procedures can be large even for simple turnings, and will be influenced by the equipment the turner can readily access. I have not attempted to explain all the chucking and sequence choices for a particular situation.

I use the terms *polish* and *polishing* for operations such as sealing, painting, varnishing, lacquering, oiling and/or waxing together with any associated sanding which are applied to the wood to enhance appearance and/or provide protection. When producing a turning, I often call the last turning operation on a workpiece *finish-turning*, a term introduced by Peter Child.[9] This term includes any appropriate sanding. Thus *finish-turning* precedes, but does not include any polishing.

I've usually taken the on-lathe photographs using an Elinchrom 250R flash head which has an exceptionally short flash duration. The resulting photographs may therefore appear posed with the lathe turned off when in fact it's running.

1.5 ENDNOTES

1. Hasluck, Paul Nooncree. *The Wood Turner's Handy Book*. London: Crosby Lockwood, 1921. (Originally published in 1887.)

2. Dunbar, Michael. *Woodturning Techniques*. Cincinnati: Popular Woodworking Books, 2017, p. 6.

3. Nish, Dale L. *Artistic Woodturning*. Provo, Utah: Brigham Young University Press, 1980, p. 23.

4. Woodham, Jonathan H. *Twentieth-Century Design*. Oxford: Oxford University Press, 1997, p. 29.

5. Regester, David. *Woodturning: Step-by-Step*. London, B.T. Batsford, 1993, p. 51.

6. Ecke, Gustav. *Chinese Domestic Furniture*. Rutland: Charles E. Tuttle, 1962, p. 28. (Originally published in 1944.)

7. Gladwell, Malcolm. *Outliers: The Story of Success*. Boston: Little, Brown, 2008.

8. Krugman, Paul. *The Great Unravelling*. London: Penguin, 2003, p. 393.

9. Child, Peter. *The Craftsman Woodturner*. London: G. Bell & Sons, 1974, p. 59.

Chapter 2

SMALL TURNING TOOLS

To turn some of the projects in this book you'll need tools with small noses. (I use *nose* to mean the sharpened edge and adjacent surfaces of any woodturning gouge, chisel or scraper.) In this chapter I discuss how to source small-nosed parting tools, skews, and detail gouges.

Manufacturers do make small-nosed tools. As figure 2.1 illustrates, their blade cross sections are usually constant along their blades' lengths and are typically scaled-down versions of the blade cross sections used for general turning. That approach too often results in blades which flex in use and thus cause catches.

Most turnings with narrow coves typically have maximum diameters less than 50 mm. Manufacturers perhaps therefore ignore the reality that their small-nosed turning tools will sometimes be used with tool overhangs considerably longer than 25 mm. Tool overhangs can be minimised by continuallly moving the toolrest forwards, but this is undesirable because it:

- cramps your tool manipulations
- slows the rate of production

- impairs you seeing both the upper and lower edges of the turning's profile so that you can readily judge and compare diameters and forms.

This chapter therefore considers how to source stiff-bladed, small-nosed versions of the main tool types, and ends by showing three diameter gauges and a calliper which you'll find ideal when turning smaller diameters.

2.1 PARTING TOOLS

Narrow parting tools are manufactured and easily ground from wider parting tools (figure 2.2). Spindles should be parted off with a skew or a parting-off tool, not a parting tool.

Figure 2.2 Four parting tools. *From left to right*: one with a "diamond" cross section 5-mm wide, one with a rectangular blade 6-mm wide and 20-mm deep, a 2-mm-wide tool, and a 6-mm-wide tool ground to give a 1.5-mm-wide cutting edge.

All are ground and honed to a 30° sharpening angle because they are cutting, not scraping, tools.

By repeatedly and slightly axially rotating a parting tool clockwise then anticlockwise as you thrust it forwards, you cut a slightly wider trench. So as not to indent the toolrest, soften the sharp edges along a parting tool's blade.

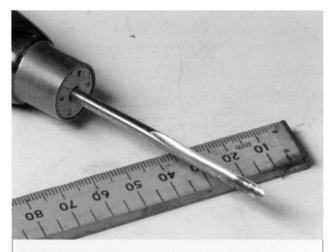

Figure 2.1 A HSS detail gouge which flexes in use. Its exposed length is 70 mm, and its diameter is 4 mm.

2.2   SKEW CHISELS

As figure 2.3 shows, turners can readily produce small skews by grinding down skews with wider-than-required blades, or by locking bits into stiff shafts. Figure 2.4 explains how I produce the latter type.

Skew chisel blades with circular cross sections are obviously stiffer than thinner, essentially rectangular blades with the same effective cutting-edge length. However when rolling tiny beads with a circular-bladed skew, the blade may have to be traversed "backwards" along the toolrest.

Figure 2.3   Two small, stiff-bladed skews, *top* 7-mm-wide, *bottom* 3-mm-wide.

Figure 2.4   Making a turning tool with a bit housed in a stiff shaft.

Here I've axially gripped in a scroll chuck a suitable length of steel cut from a 10-mm-diameter mild steel bolt or machine screw. After scraping a small axial recess in the right-hand end of the shaft to accurately center the drill tip, I bored a hole about 25-mm long. The drill's diameter should be such that the bit will fit snugly within the hole.   **>**

> For a tiny skew, I use the unfluted part of a HSS twist drill as the bit. For tiny gouges, the bit can be cut from a too-slender gouge shaft such as that shown next to the bedway. I use the edge of a grinding wheel to cut off a bit length.
>
> To lock the bit into the bored hole you could use a suitable adhesive. Instead I usually just use a crisp blow with a hammer on the end of the shaft as shown on the right-hand gouge in figure 2.12.

2.3   DETAIL GOUGES

Detail gouges are extensively used with both axially and transversely grained workpieces. As figure 2.1 shows, smaller sizes are commonly fitted with blades which flex. To overcome this, I'll first consider detail gouge blade cross sections, then how to grind their noses.

Figure 2.5 shows the ideal detail gouge cross section. Before HSS displaced carbon tool steel, for cutting deep narrow coves, narrow blades with cross sections similar to that shown in figure 2.6 were produced by forging. The resulting blades were rotationally unstable, required more complicated manipulations, and in some cases were still not stiff enough.

Properly-stiff, small-fluted HSS gouges could be created by manufacturers producing detail-gouge blades with cross sections similar to that shown in figure 2.7. I'm not aware that such gouges are currently manufactured. Turners can however produce satisfactory alternatives by:

1. grinding down the nose of a suitable bowl gouge with an effectively small flute radius (this is detailed on pages 15 and 16). Manufactured bowl gouges usually have U- or parabola-shaped flute cross sections and high flanges. Their blades are therefore considerably stiffer than those of detail gouges with the same blade diameter. Also the cross section of the bottom of most bowl gouge flutes is close to semicircular
2. cutting a too-slender blade shorter—you then have the option of using the off-cut as a bit
3. cutting a slender blade into short lengths (bits) which are fixed into stiff shafts as explained in figure 2.4.

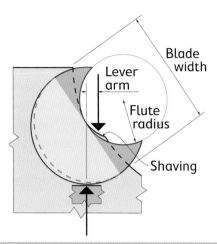

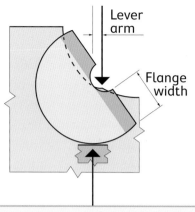

Figure 2.5 The optimum, rotationally-stable detail gouge cross section. The smaller the lever arm between the force exerted by the shaving and the upward reaction force exerted by the toolrest, the smaller the tool's tendency to unexpectedly rotate and catch. This lever arm is small when there is a semicircle of steel below the base of the flute. Because most cutting is performed by the cutting edge's shoulders, the lever arm is even smaller if the semicircle is slightly flattened (indicated by the blue, dashed line).

Obviously the stiffness of a blade with this cross section is related to its width.

Figure 2.7 A rotationally-stable, stiff blade cross section with a small flute radius. To improve its ability to cut deep, narrow coves, the nose's width must be reduced by grinding back the flanges as shown in figures 2.10 and 2.11.

2.3.1 Detail gouge noses

There's less tear-out if you cut cove bottoms with the gouge's active edge (the length of edge actively cutting) presented at about 45° side rake (skewed at about 45° to the velocity of the wood about to be cut). Therefore of the two gouge noses shown in figure 2.8, the ladyfinger nose at the top is far better than the fingernail nose at the bottom. However if you grind a basic ladyfinger nose like that in figure 2.8 on a bowl gouge or on a blade

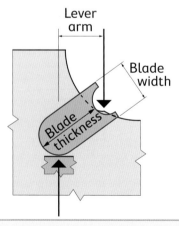

Figure 2.6 A blade cross section which is somewhat stiffer than one with the same flute radius but the figure 2.5 cross section. However this deeper blade cross section results in a longer lever arm between the two forces and therefore greater rotational instability.

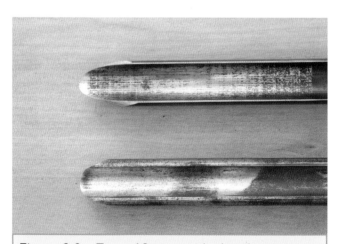

Figure 2.8 *Top*, a 19-mm-wide detail gouge with a ladyfinger nose; *bottom*, a gouge with a fingernail nose.

with a cross section similar to that shown in figure 2.7, you'll only be able to cut narrow coves a little deeper than semicircular. To cut much deeper narrow coves without lessening the blade's cross section back from the nose, you need to reduce:

- the sharpening angle
- the height of the flanges in the nose region
- the width of the nose

The effectiveness of reducing the sharpening angle and the height of a blade's flanges at the nose end of the blade is explained in figure 2.9. Nose grindings which enable the flange height and nose width are shown in figure 2.10. The three types of resulting gouge noses are shown in figures 2.11 and 2.12.

The grinding to reduce nose flange heights and widths can be done on a conventional bench grinder with the blade's axis parallel to the velocity of the grinding wheel's periphery or parallel to the grinder's spindle.

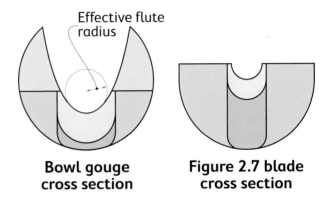

Effective flute radius

Bowl gouge cross section   **Figure 2.7 blade cross section**

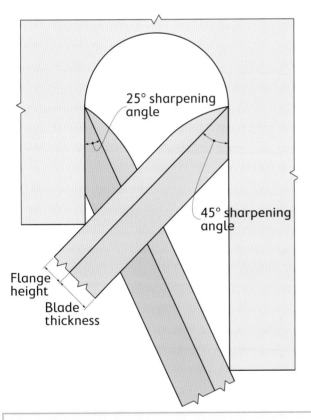

25° sharpening angle

45° sharpening angle

Flange height

Blade thickness

Figure 2.9 Showing that the depth of cove which a gouge can cut without fouling the cove rim increases as the sharpening angle decreases. Therefore sharpen detail gouges at 25°. Also, the smaller the sum of the flange height and blade thickness beneath the bottom of the flute, the deeper the cove which can be cut.

Figure 2.10 Grinding noses on stiff blades to allow the tools to cut deep, narrow coves. The unground cross section has a mauve fill. The outlines with the palest, medium and darkest orange fills represent respectively grinding down the flanges, grinding away nose width, and grinding the nose's cross section below the bottom of the flute to a semicircle. This third grinding operation is usually optional because the area of the blade which is usually being supported by the toolrest is well back from the nose.

Figure 2.11 A 9.5-mm-wide gouge blade with a flute radius of 1.75 mm, a blade cross section similar to that in figure 2.7. The nose has been ground as shown on the right-hand side of figure 2.10.

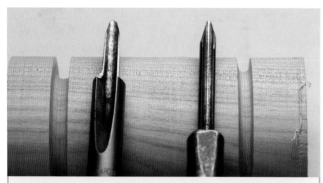

Figure 2.12 The noses of two adequately stiff, small-fluted gouges sharpened with ladyfinger noses, and a cove cut by each.

Left, the flute radius of the modified bowl gouge is 2.5 mm, and the cove is 5.5-mm-wide and 9-mm-deep. *Right*, the blade width of the inserted bit is 6 mm, and its flute radius is 1.5 mm. The cove is 4.5-mm wide and 5-mm deep. The flat on the top of the shaft in which the bit is housed results from a hammer blow to lock the bit into the bored hole in the shaft.

Figure 2.13 Hones for small-nosed turning tools. *Left to right*: a Norton FS-24 aluminium oxide India slipstone, a diamond-coated slipstone with slightly larger edge radii, a super-fine-grained diamond file, and a coarse-grained diamond file.

2.4   SHARPENING, HANDLES AND CALLIPERS

Small turning tools need gentler sharpening, and seem more responsive if they're fitted with lighter handles. The smaller the workpiece, the more apparent small errors in diameter become, and the greater the importance of accurate callipering. This section discusses these three topics.

2.4.1   Sharpening small turning tools

Although a high-speed (3,000 rpm) grinder with, say, an 80-grit wheel is fine for approximate shaping of small woodturning tool noses, it's rather aggressive for regrinding. A slow-speed grinder with a finer, say 120- or 160-grit wheel would be better. If, like me, you don't have this facility, a coarse diamond file can be employed for refining the nose form before honing with a fine-grained diamond file or slip stone. (As Alan Lacer and Jeryl Wright have shown in their article "Does Honing Pay Off?", diamond is the preferred honing abrasive for

HSS because of the presence of very hard nonferrous carbides in the steel.)[1] Diamond-coated slipstones are available, but you'll probably have to source an aluminium oxide (figure 2.13) or silicon carbide slipstone for honing flutes with very small radiuses.

2.4.2   Handles for small turning tools

I prefer that my small-nosed turning tools not be appreciably shorter than those used for general turning, and that their handles be a little slimmer than usual (figure 2.14). I prefer wooden handles to metal because my workshop is cold in the winter. Also I don't like my handle surfaces to be smooth or highly polished because I then have to grip them more tightly which inhibits easy manipulation. Therefore if I'm "improving" a manufacturer's handle, even if I haven't appreciably slimmed it, I produce the finished surface using a small roughing gouge presented without side rake. I then don't sand this surface.

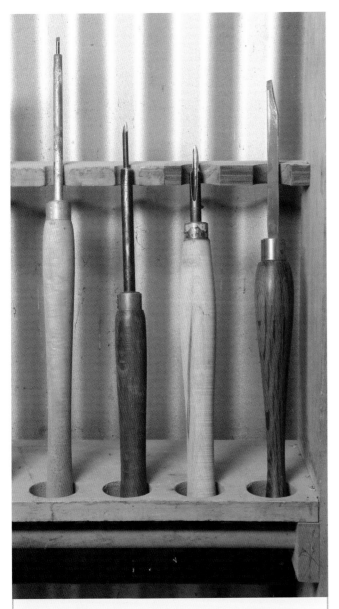

Figure 2.14 Four small-nosed tools. The two paler handles have been turned down and left unsanded, my current preference.

The design of the tool rack in which the handle ends are supported on a dowel was shown in my first woodturning book *The Practice of Woodturning*.[2]

2.4.3 Callipers

Figure 2.15 shows three fixed-diameter gauges, and a vernier calliper which you'll find especially useful for smaller items which have several different diameters which you want to calliper.

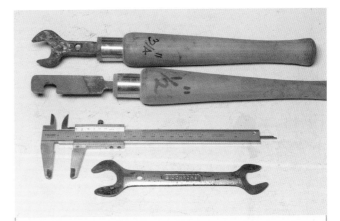

Figure 2.15 A vernier calliper and three fixed-diameter gauges.

Look for a brand of vernier calliper which has a large and strong locking knob. Mine has both imperial and metric rulings.

I've filed the inside corners of the calliper's and gauges' jaws round so that the jaws don't grab as the desired diameter is achieved.

2.5 ENDNOTES

1. Lacer, Alan and Wright, Jeryl. "Does Honing Pay Off?". pp. 58–63. *Sharpening Turning Tools*. St Paul: American Association of Woodturners, 2014.

2. Darlow, Mike. *The Practice of Woodturning*. Sydney: The Melaleuca Press, 1985, p. 40.

A BACKSCRATCHER

I hope that readers will accept that the subject of this project chapter does not imply that the personal hygiene or domestic cleanliness of readers is in any way deficient.

Design

The backscratcher design pictured in figures 3.1 and 3.2 has two desirable features:

1. As demonstrated in figure 3.3, the itch can be relieved when the person is dressed because the backscratcher's head is compact, and its flattened side won't catch on clothing. Figure 3.2 shows an optional modification which may make the implement easier to slide down a clothed back.

2. The "scratchiness" can be varied according to how much you round the head's rib edges by sanding.

Making

This back scratcher is a simple spindle turning. A strong, fine-grained hardwood is ideal. I used silver ash, which can be either of the two Australian species *Flindersia bourjotiana* and *Flindersia schottiana*. (The genus name recalls Matthew Flinders whose chess set is featured in chapter 5.)

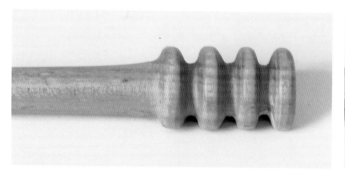

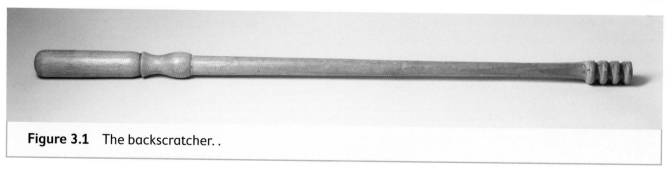

Figure 3.1 The backscratcher. .

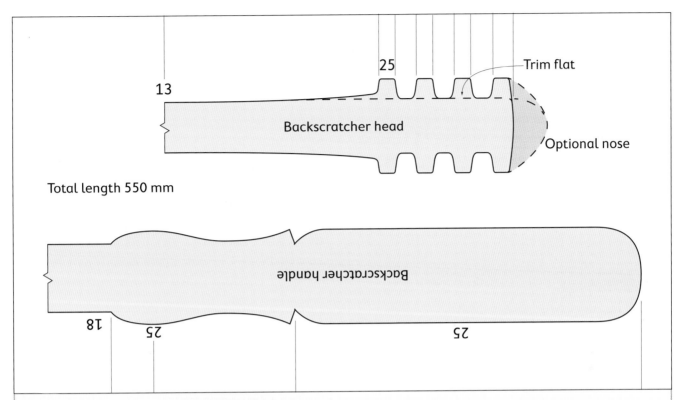

Figure 3.2 The pencil gauge for the backscratcher. One improvement, shown dashed, might be to include a nose at the end of the head so that the head will more easily slide inside one's clothing. Instead of having a straight taper, the shaft will look better if it is slightly swollen (has entasis like the shaft of a classical column).

Figure 3.3 The backscratcher in use.

MAKING CHESSMEN

This chapter is a general introduction to making chessmen. Chapters 5 and 6 then cover the background, design and making of particular chess sets, all but two of which do not appear in my 2004 book *Turned Chessmen*, later retitled in the United States as *Woodturning Chessmen*.

Making a chess set involves:

- designing the pieces, deciding the chucking, and preparing the gauges
- selecting the woods and preparing the individual workpieces for turning
- turning, including any boring. Sourcing the small woodturning tools which you may need is discussed in this book's chapter 2.

It can also involve:

- polishing
- installing the leading
- leathering.

4.1 CHUCKING WORKPIECES FOR LEADED CHESSMEN

Oxford dictionaries define a *chuck* as a 'holding device, typically one with jaws which "move radially in and out"'. In woodturning a wider definition has long been the norm. Thus cupchucks and screwchucks which don't have any moving parts; and drive centers, dead and live tail centers, and faceplates are also regarded as chucks. Therefore workpieces held between centers in a woodturning lathe and those fixed onto a headstock spindle nose using some form of chuck which may not have any moveable jaws can be said to be *chucked*.

Chessmen can be separated into leaded and unleaded. Leaded men are heavier, more stable, and more satisfying to play with, but many chess set designs don't have sufficiently bulky bottom ends to accept leading. The lead is typically housed in an axial hole bored into the

bottom of the man. This hole is best bored before the man is finish-turned—were the leading hole bored after finish-turning the hole is unlikely to be truly axial and the man's surface would probably be damaged by being gripped.

Turned Chessmen shows twelve chucking methods on pages 132 and 133. Its method J screwchuck is shown in figure 4.1 below. I have recently developed the improved chucking method shown in figures 4.2 to 4.4.

Figure 4.1 A 1/2"-diameter screw chuck. The length of steel rod with a 1/2"-BSW (British Standard Whitworth) thread is locked into a faceplate similar to that shown in figures 4.3 and 4.4.

The lower photograph shows the chuck's construction. The right-hand piece of wood illustrates how a workpiece is gripped by the thread. Alternatively, as shown in figure 4.2, you could hold the threaded rod in a scroll chuck.

Figure 4.2   A loose-pin chuck held in an engineers scroll chuck. The loose pin is hacksawn from a nail.

Figure 4.4   The loose-pin chuck drawn in figure 4.3.

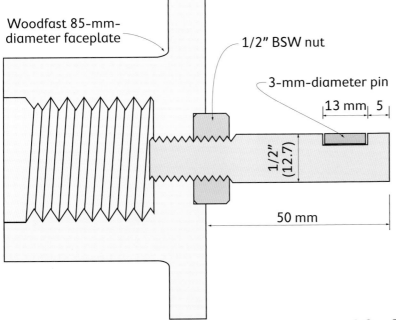

Woodfast 85-mm-diameter faceplate

1/2" BSW nut

3-mm-diameter pin

13 mm   5

1/2" (12.7)

50 mm

Figure 4.3   A 1/2"-diameter loose-pin chuck. The rod is cut from a screw, and has a 1/2" BSW thread which screws into an axial hole with the same thread in the Woodfast-brand faceplate. The diameter of the leading hole (here 1/2") should be such that the rod is a snug fit within. To lock the workpiece onto the chuck, twist the workpiece clockwise (looking towards the headstock).

4.2   BORING THE LEADING HOLE

If a chessman workpiece has been prepared with a flat top and bottom whose surfaces are perpendicular to the man's longitudinal axis, the leading hole can be bored in a drilling machine. Otherwise turn blanks between centers to produce multiple or single chessman workpieces, each with a chucking spigot (figures 4.5 or 4.6 respectively). Chuck each workpiece by its chucking spigot, cut the bottom very slightly concave, and bore the leading hole as shown in figures 4.7 to 4.10.

Figure 4.5   A workpiece turned into three workpieces, each with a chucking spigot at its right-hand end.

Figure 4.6   A single chessman workpiece ready for chucking by the chucking spigot at its right-hand end.

Figure 4.7   Chucking the workpiece in a scroll chuck, here with dovetail jaws.

Figure 4.8   Flatting the bottom of the chessman slightly concave. The skew's long point is being pushed slowly forwards in a shallow arc by my left hand (I'm right-handed).

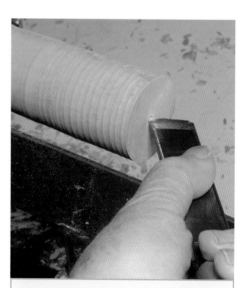

Figure 4.9   Scraping a small conical recess with a skew's long point to center the point of the drill so that the boring will be truly axial.

Figure 4.10 Boring the workpiece with a 1/2"-diameter drill. The yellow tape is a depth gauge.

Figure 4.12 Chucking a king workpiece on the 1/2" screwchuck shown in figure 4.1. The headstock spindle is locked, and the tail center is wound forward to keep the workpiece in axial alignment as the workpiece is screwed to the left.

The bored hole needs to be just large enough in diameter so that the screw thread bites. If the hole diameter is too small, the workpiece is too hard to screw on and off: if too large, the thread won't grip the workpiece securely.

Figure 4.11 Chucking the workpiece on a 1/2"-diameter loose pin chuck.

The yellow tape on the chuck rim indicates where the flat in the rod is so that when dechucking the workpiece by twisting it anticlockwise, the loose pin can be on top of the chuck's flat, and therefore less likely to fall down. If it does, it will be caught by the tray.

4.3 CHUCKING CHESSMEN WORKPIECES

Whether a chessman workpiece has been bored for leading is likely to affect how you decide to chuck that workpiece for finish-turning and polishing.

If a set's men won't be leaded, they can be turned between centers, or cantilevered from a chuck, usually with the men's bottoms to the left so that their tops can be fully finish-turned in the lathe.

If a set will be bored for leading, and you'll use either of the chucking methods shown in figures 4.11 and 4.12, this will dictate the diameter and minimum depth of the leading hole. Other chucking methods for leaded chessmen include:

- After boring as in figure 4.10, don't de-chuck the workpiece for finish-turning. It's best to use the nose of a preferably live tail center to provide additional support.
- Mount the workpiece between centers.

Other factors which could influence your choices of the sequences of operations and chucking methods are:

- whether it's preferable to complete each man separately, or perform each operation on all the men before performing the next operation on all the men. For example, if you choose the former approach you might have to repeatedly swap between a drill and a live center in the tailstock swallow
- the chucks, range of drill diameters, and other equipment which you can access
- how you polish the men. If some or all of the polishing operations are best done in the lathe, this may cause you to delay parting-off.

4.4 POLISHING

I don't have a spraying facility. Also I prefer a gloss finish for chessmen, but not one of perceptible thickness. Because it has no color tint, the polish I prefer is water-based polyurethane.

After a set has been finish-turned, I apply one coat with a brush with the workpiece rotating slowly in the lathe to each man. After the polish has hardened, I sand-back almost to the wood, again with the workpiece chucked in the lathe. I then apply a friction polish such as Shellawax in the lathe. Because I use the lathe for polishing operations, I lead after polishing.

4.5 LEADING

Chess sets are normally leaded (weighted) with lead because its specific gravity is 11.3 (that of iron is about 7.1). Leading is done after the turning, sanding and polishing are completed.

Sheet lead is obtainable from plumbing suppliers. Lead melts at 327.5 °C. You can therefore melt it in an old saucepan on the hob or ring of a domestic stove. Lead vapor is poisonous, so do this in a very well ventilated location or, better, outdoors. Also, unless the wood is fully seasoned, when you pour molten lead into the leading hole, you're likely to get a dangerous Roman-candle-like eruption of molten lead droplets.

For my sets I now therefore prefer to lead with a "mortar" of lead shot (obtainable from gun smiths) and cross-linked PVA, epoxy resin, or another suitable glue

with gap-filling ability. After inverting the men in a rack (figure 4.13), and coating the wall of a hole with the glue, I then press the mortar into the leading hole, taking care that it doesn't stand proud of the bottom (figure 4.14).

Figure 4.13 A rack to hold inverted chessmen for leading.

Figure 4.14 Leading with lead shot and cross-linked PVA glue. The lead is being ladled into the bored holes with a teaspoon which has been squashed in a vice to form a spout. I do the leading over a shallow tray to contain any spilled lead shot.

4.6   LEATHERING

Leaded sets are usually leathered with thin leather (best), felt or baize. You can punch out the disks of material— punches (figure 4.15) are available in a wide range of diameters, but are expensive to buy. I instead prefer to turn the disks as shown in figures 4.16 and 4.17. I then glue the disks onto the men's bottoms with PVA.

Figure 4.17   Turning the leather squares to their finished diameter. So as to cut with high side rake I'm using the cutting edge at the shoulder of a detail gouge.

Figure 4.15   Leather punches.

Figure 4.16   Chucking squares of thin leather between two wooden mandrels whose adjacent free ends have been turned to the required finished diameter of the leather disks. One of the adjacent mandrel faces is slightly concave so that the leather squares are held securely at their intended diameter.

Chapter 5

THREE ANTIQUE CHESS SETS

After my book *Turned Chessmen* was published in 2004, I didn't refocus on chess set design and making until I read of the July 2012 sale by Sotheby's of a single 6.7-cm-high walrus ivory queen carved in about 1400 AD for £277,250. This spectacular Sotheby's sale was later eclipsed by two others: in July 2019 one of the five missing Lewis chessmen not in the British Museum or National Museum of Scotland sold for £735,000, and in July 2020 a Gothic walrus ivory king thought to represent Holy Roman Emperor Frederick II (1194-1250) sold for £653,000. Unfortunately none of my own chessmen have achieved similar prices.

The preceding chapter covered some general aspects of making chessmen. This chapter first reintroduces chess set signatures and symbols before focussing on three antique sets.

5.1 SIGNATURES AND SYMBOLS

To appreciate my comments on the designs of chess sets you'll need to understand the concepts of set, side and piece signatures and piece symbols which I introduced in *Turned Chessmen*.

A chess set has 32 chessmen divided into two sides. Each side consists of specific numbers of each of six pieces. A *set signature* consists of the 'features which identify preferably all the men of a set as belonging to that set'. The *side signature* 'identifies which side in the set a chessman belongs to'—in the majority of sets the side signatures are particular colors. Hence the two sides are usually called *black* and *white* even when the side signatures aren't those two colors or aren't colors at all. The *piece signature* identifies a chessman as being one of the six pieces. Piece signatures often consist of two features: the relative height of the piece, and what I call a *piece symbol* such as a miter for a bishop or a castle tower for a rook. The piece name abbreviations are: king (K), queen (Q), bishop (B), knight (N), rook (R), and pawn

(P). In this book's illustrations of chess sets the pieces are shown in this order starting from the left.

5.2 THE ROWBOTHUM SET

Figure 5.1 shows an almost exact copy of the original antique set, details of which were sent to me by a member of Chess Collectors International, a society of chess set collectors. I've named the design *Rowbothum*. Why will be explained shortly. The set is English. It's age is uncertain, but it's most likely to be 17th century.

The Rowbothum set's design is in the St George style. This style name, coined long after the Rowbothum set was made, recalls a set design used by the St George's Chess Club which was founded in 1843 and first met at Beattie's Hotel on the corner of George Street and Cavendish Square in London. The characteristics of this pattern are a fairly cylindrical overall form with a wealth of detail including high beads and half beads, deep coves, prominent V-cuts, and strong piece signatures. Several different nineteenth-century St George sets are shown at *www.chess-museum.com/st-george-chessmen. html*.

As figure 5.1 shows, the Rowbothum design is without a simple and consistent set signature. Therefore, although design improvement, and especially rationalisation, is a focus of mine, the forms of the Rowbothum pieces below their piece symbols are so gloriously confused that I haven't attempted to redesign them.

Five of the Rowbothum set's finial piece signatures are conventional: a king's crown, a queen's orb, a bishop's miter, and a sphere for a pawn (foot soldier). Two piece symbols are however uncommon: the knight's and the rook's.

The knight's piece symbol may represent a pot helm (figure 5.2), but if so why the bevelled face? This face could represent either a heater-shaped (like that of the sole of a clothes iron) shield or the front view of a charger's head. Another possibility is found in Randle Holme's

Academy of Armoury of 1681–2: "The Knights are the pins which haue their heads cut aslant like a feather in a helmet".[1]

The first chess book printed in England, and only the second book to be printed in England, was Caxton's 1474 *The Game and Playe of the Chesse*. Damiano's *Questo libro e da imparare giocare a scachi* published in Rome in 1512 is the second-oldest extant printed chess book. A French translation was published in Paris in 1560, and this French version was translated into English and published in London in 1562 by James Rowbothum. The extract below from Rowbothum's book is quoted from Harold J. R. Murray's *A History of Chess* published in 1913:[2]

Our Englishe Cheastmen are commonly made nothing like vnto these foresayde fashions: to wit, the King is made the highest or longest: the Queene is longest nexte vnto him: the Bishoppe is made with a sharp toppe and clouen in the middest not much vnlyke to a bishops Myter: the knight hath his top cut aslope, as thoughe beynge dubbed knight: the Rooke is made lykest to the kinge, and the Queene, but that he is not so long: the

Figure 5.2   A pot helm.
   Scanned from: Fox-Davies, Arthur Charles. *A Complete Guide to Heraldry*. London: T.C. & E.C. Jack, 1909, p. 307.

Figure 5.1   The pieces of the Rowbothum design. The knight is shown in front and side elevation. The darker wood is blackwood (*Acacia melanoxylon*) , the paler wood is silver wattle (*Acacia dealbata*).

Paunes be made smalest and least of all, and thereby they may best be knowen.

However unless the knight's dubbing was ill-directed and far more forceful than usual, this explanation, like Holme's "feather in a helmet", isn't an entirely convincing.

The Rowbothum rook's piece symbol is a sphere rather than the usual representation of a castle tower. The reference in Rowbothum's book that "the Rooke . . . is made lykest to the . . . Queene" suggests that the spherical rook piece symbol was in use in the 17th century. This is confirmed by the statement in Francis Beale's *The Royall Game of Chesse-Play*, published in London in 1656, that "the Rook is sometimes fashioned with a round head, sometimes like a castle".[3] The use of a spherical rook piece symbol continued: a 19th-century and more sophisticated St George design with sphere-topped rooks is shown at *exeterchessclub.org.uk/content/ st-george-chess-set-turned-wood.*

5.2.1 Design

Figure 5.3 provides pencil gauges for the original six pieces. Figure 5.4 shows a gauge for a substitute rook R_{RB} with a battlement. You could hollow the top of this rook and carve embrasures (explained in figure 5.5) to better define the battlement.

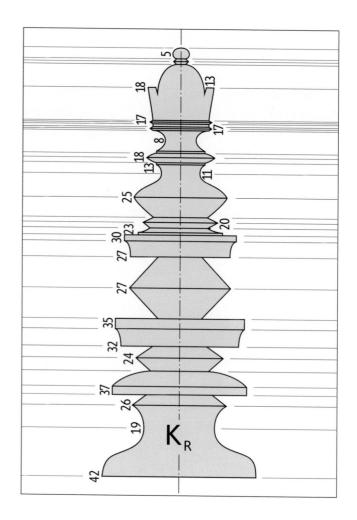

Figure 5.3   Pencil gauges for the original six Rowbothum pieces are shown in the following six diagrams.

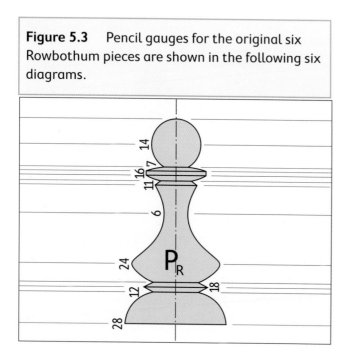

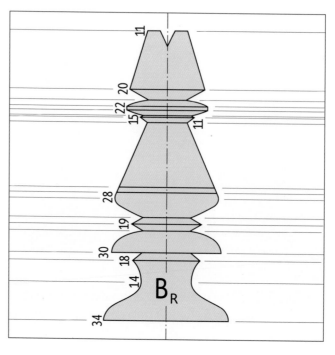

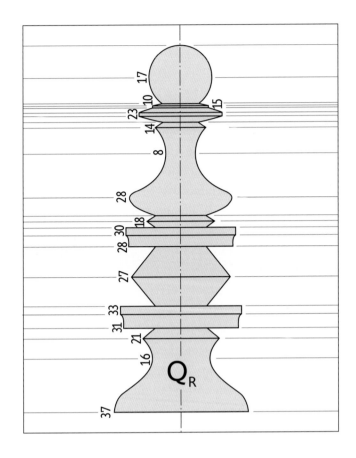

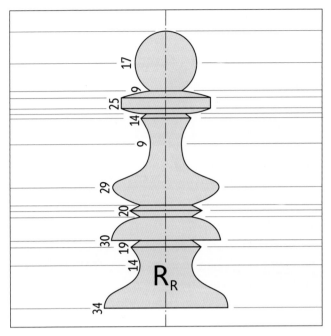

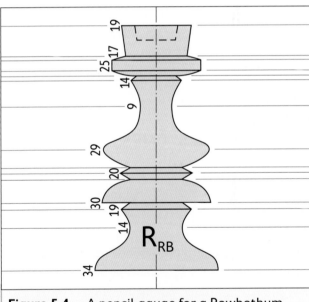

Figure 5.4 A pencil gauge for a Rowbothum rook variant with a battlement.

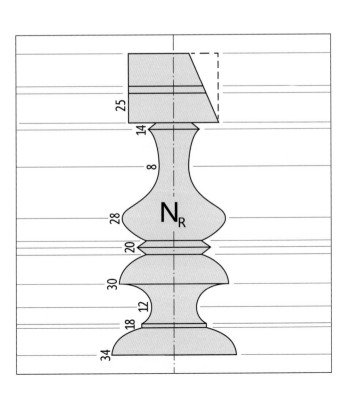

5.2.2 Making

The original set would have need turned between centers. If you do the same, decide whether you'll accept a poppet recess in the finished top, or whether to include waste length in the workpieces to allow for parting off and hand finishing. If you want to hollow the tops of the R_{RB} rooks, you'll need to chuck their workpieces by their bottom ends.

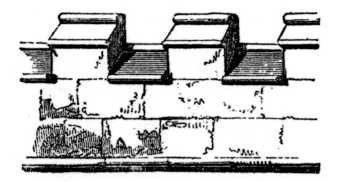

Figure 5.5 The nomenclature of battlements. This illustration shows the decorative battlement of Saint Mary's church, Beverly, Yorkshire. The upstanding elements are called *merlons*. The gaps between merlons are called *embrasures*, but when wider than the merlons are called *crenels* or *crenelles*.

Scanned from: Sturgis, Russell et al. *Sturgis' Illustrated Dictionary of Architecture and Building*. Mineola: Dover Publications, 1989, Vol I, column 247. (Originally published 1901–02.)

5.3 FLINDERS' CHESS SET

I've lived a third of my life in England and two thirds in Australia. The chess set pictured in figure 5.6 is therefore particularly interesting to me because it belonged to Matthew Flinders, shown in figure 5.7, the Englishman who commanded the second circumnavigation of Australia and surveyed its coastline. (The first circumnavigation of Australia was made in 1642-3 by the ships *Heemskerck* and *Zeehaen* under the command of Abel Tasman. During that voyage he discovered the island now named after him, but did not even glimpse the Australian mainland.) But before discussing Flinders' chess set, I'll outline his life.

5.3.1 Flinders' life

Born in 1774, Matthew Flinders was sixteen when he embarked on his naval career as a midshipman aboard the *Scipio*. In 1791 he sailed under Captain William Bligh to the South Pacific, returning in 1793. In 1794

Flinders, on board the *Bellerophon*, took part in the blockade of Revolutionary France, and in the battle of The Glorious First of June, also against France. Thomas Pasley, Flinders' first patron, lost a leg in this battle.

In 1795 Flinders grabbed the opportunity to sail to New South Wales on the *Reliance* with the new Governor, Captain John Hunter. The surgeon on the *Reliance* was George Bass, and he and Flinders became firm friends.

By that time Australia's east coast had been charted by Cook, but not in detail, and the coast close to Port Jackson (the name Cook gave Sydney harbor) had been explored by Hunter in 1788 and 1789. Bass and Flinders, keen to explore further, first set out from Sydney (named in 1788) in a 3-meter-long boat from the *Reliance* which they called *Tom Thumb*. (A replica of *Tom Thumb* is in the Australian National Maritime Museum in Sydney.) With Bass's young servant, they sailed through Sydney Heads, south into Botany Bay, and up the George's River. This nine-day exploration led to the founding of Banks Town (named after Sir Joseph Banks) in which Bass and Flinders were each granted 100 acres in 1798.

At that time, vessels reached Sydney from the Cape of Good Hope by sailing around the south of Tasmania and up its east coast because Tasmania was believed to be part of mainland Australia.

After an abortive attempt by Bass to prove or disprove this belief, Flinders and Bass, on the *Norfolk*, settled the matter by circumnavigating Tasmania, returning to Sydney on 12 January 1799. Flinders suggested the strait be named after Bass. His report was sent to England, published, and came to the attention of Banks.

When Flinders returned to England, he prepared charts and an account of his explorations; he also married Ann Chappelle on 17 April 1801. Their time together was short for after successfully lobbying Banks, Flinders was commissioned to chart and explore the Australian coastline. He sailed from Spithead, the estuary south of Portsmouth, on the *Investigator* on 18 July 1801.

On 22 July 1802, the *Investigator* sailed north from Sydney and circumnavigated Australia. After this the *Investigator* was no longer seaworthy. Flinders therefore attempted to return England on the *Porpoise*, but it was wrecked on a reef off the Queensland coast. Managing

Figure 5.6 Flinders' chess set and its box. The sides' woods are boxwood (*Buxus sempervirens*) and a rosewood (*Dalbergia* species). The set was probably given to Flinders in Mauritius by his friend Mr Labauve on 1 April 1810. In this photograph the bishops and knights are transposed from their normal positions.

Flinders' wife Ann gave birth to their only child Anne on 1 April 1812. Anne married, becoming Anne Flinders Petrie. This set was donated to Mitchell Library, part of the State Library of New South Wales, by descendent Lady Flinders Petrie in 1949.

Courtesy of the State Library of New South Wales.

Figure 5.7 A watercolor portrait of Matthew Flinders painted on ivory in 1801.

Courtesy of the State Library of New South Wales.

to get back to Sydney, Flinders took command of the *Cumberland*, and again sailed for England.

This ship, too, was in poor state, and Flinders, being unaware that France and Britain were again at war, put into Port Louis, the capital of Île de France (now called Mauritius), on 17 December 1803 for repairs.

Mauritius is an island of volcanic origins in the Indian Ocean (figure 5.8). Its length and width are each about 28 km. It was the home of the dodo, shown in figure 5.9. These birds were slaughtered into extinction by 1681. Mauritius was also rich in ebony.

Mauritius was discovered by Arab sailors in about 975. The Portuguese first landed there in 1507, but did little to exploit its resources, and abandoned it after about 90 years. The Dutch seized the island in 1598, named it after Prince Maurice, Prince of Orange and Count of Nassau (1567-1625), but in turn abandoned it in 1710. The French occupied it between 1715 and 1810, and called it the Île de France—the capital is still called Port Louis. Britain then occupied the island in 1810 in order to expel the privateers who were preying on British shipping. Britain took formal possession by the 1814 Treaty of Paris. Mauritius became independent in 1968.

France had developed Port Louis as a naval base and the then French governor, General Charles Decaen, held

Flinders on Mauritius for six and a half years. It was during his time there that Flinders acquired his chess set. Flinders was released and left Mauritius on 13 June 1810 on the *Harriet*.

Flinders arrived in England in October 1810. The Admiralty agreed to assist him to publish an account of his voyages. Flinders died on 19 July, 1814, but had lived to see his *A Voyage to Terra Australis* printed.

Flinders, aged 40, was buried on 23 July 1814 in St James's burial ground in London. When closed, this burial ground held the remains of about 60,000 people. In January 2019 during excavations for the HS2 high-speed rail project at Euston Station, Flinders' lead breast plate was found and allowed his remains to be identified for a fitting reburial.[4]

Flinders is deservedly the subject of recent biographies by Ernest Scott, Miriam Estensen, Rob Mundle

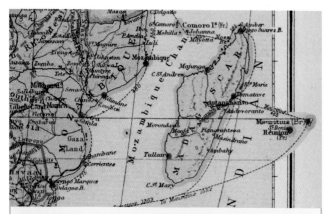

Figure 5.8 The location of Mauritius in the western Indian Ocean.. The distance from the African coast to Mauritius along the 30°-south latitude is 2600 km (1,600 miles).

Scanned from *The New Pictorial Atlas of the World*: London, Odhams Press, no date.

Figure 5.9 A somewhat less glamorous dodo than that usually illustrated, here painted circa 1602 by Jacob Hoefnagel (1573-1632/33) from a live dodo in the menagerie of Emperor Rudolph II in Prague.

Sourced from Wikimedia Commons.

and Kenneth Morgan.[5,6,7,8] He is commemorated in the name of the tree genus *Flindersia*, and in the names of many Australian locations and institutions including Flinders Street Station in Melbourne, the town of Flinders in Victoria, The Flinders Ranges, Flinders University in South Australia, and Flinders Island in Bass Strait.

Only a little less famous than Flinders is his black and white cat Trim. Trim was born in 1799 aboard the *Reliance* while it was anchored at Cape Town. He was named after a manservant in Laurence Sterne's novel *Tristram Shandy* published between 1759 and 1767. This manservant showed "great fidelity and affection" towards his master.[9] Trim disappeared in Mauritius in 1804. This prompted Flinders to write the short book *A Biographical Tribute to the Memory of Trim*. He took the manuscript to England, but made no attempt to publish it. The book has since been published several times. Bryce Courtenay, also wrote a book about Trim,[9] and he (Trim) has been sculpted at least three times (figure 5.10).[10]

5.3.2 William Flinders Petrie

Flinders and his wife Anne had one child, a daughter also named Anne. She married William Petrie, and their son William Matthew Flinders Petrie was born in 1853. Shown in figure 5.11, he became an important archeologist and Egyptologist. In 1905 in the western Sinai Flinders Petrie and his wife Hilda stumbled across inscriptions which were later identified as probably the original alphabetic script.[11] Flinders Petrie was knighted in 1923, and died in Jerusalem in 1942.

Figure 5.11   William Matthew Flinders Petrie in 1903.
Courtesy of the Petrie Museum of Egyptian Archeology. UCL.

5.3.3 The design of Flinders' chess set

Flinders' chess set is a commercial French Régence set of the late 18th century. Figure 5.12 shows my replicas of the pieces. Figure 5.13 shows a slightly different version from around the same time. Other Régence sets are pictured in *Master Pieces*[12] and *Chessmen Art and History*.[13] A further version was owned by Benjamin Franklin (1706–1790). His chess article "The Morals of Chess", published in the *Columbian* magazine in 1786, was the first to be published in the United States of America.[14]

Figure 5.10   A bronze sculpture of Trim on the western side of the State Library of New South Wales.

Figure 5.12   Replicas of the Flinders' chess pieces turned in blackwood (*Acacia melanoxylon*). On the right are an "improved" bishop with a more defined miter and an "improved" knight cut aslant. The men of Flinders' original set are small: its kings are only 85-mm high. I therefore made these pieces 50% bigger than the originals.

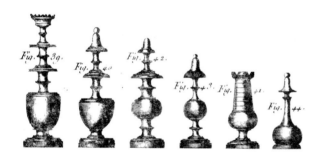

Figure 5.13   Régence pieces similar to those of Flinders' set.

    Rearranged after being scanned from: Hamelin-Bergeron, Pierre. *Manuel du Tourneur*, 2nd edition. 1816, Vol I, plate XXV.

The Régence piece signatures don't resemble those of the now dominant Staunton design (shown later in figure 6.1). To today's players therefore the design of the Flinders set suffers from several shortcomings and compromises:

- There are three different set signatures in the Flinders' set: the urn of the king, queen and rook; the oblate spheroid of the bishop and knight; and the oblate spheroid on a thumb mould of the pawn.

- Piece heights usually aid piece identification. However the heights of the Flinders' set's king and queen are similar, and although shorter, so are the heights of the bishop and knight.

- In Régence sets the piece symbol of the bishop doesn't attempt to represent a bishop's miter. Perhaps the thimble-like form atop the Flinders' bishops represents some other type of clerical headwear.

- In many Régence sets, including Flinders', the knight's piece symbol isn't an expensive-to-carve charger's head and neck. Instead it's a turned finial which is usually carved with three facets to represent

Figure 5.14 "Portrait of a man in a tricorn hat" painted by John Russell (1745-1806) in the collection of the Art Institute of Chicago. Sourced from Wikimedia Commons.

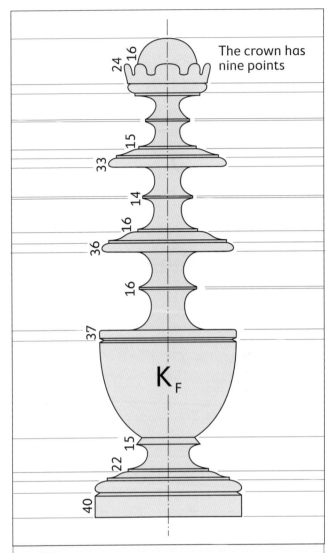

The crown has nine points

Figure 5.15 This and the following five gauges are for pieces which are 50% bigger than those of Flinders' original set.

a tricorn hat (figure 5.14). When the knight has the charger piece symbol, the bishop may have two facets which according to Mathieu and Ine Kloprogge represent that "the influence of the clergy was waning".[15] Note that in figure 1.31 of *Turned Chessmen* which shows the pieces of another Régence set, the bishop and knight are transposed; thus the knight is third from the left and the bishop third from the right.

- to avoid 18th-century turners having to cantilever the rook workpieces from a cupchuck, the tops of the rooks aren't recessed to represent a tower top with a parapet. Also the carving of the embrasure representations is perfunctory.

Figure 5.15 comprises the pencil gauges to replicate the Flinders' set. Figure 5.16 shows an alternative "improved" bishop and knight in which:

- the piece signature of the bishop is a miter (which beneficially makes the bishop taller),
- the knight's piece signature is a pot helm cut aslant.

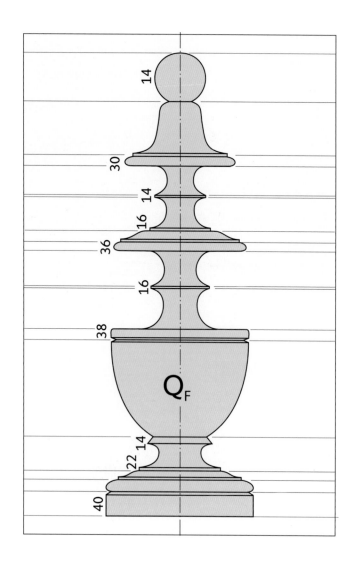

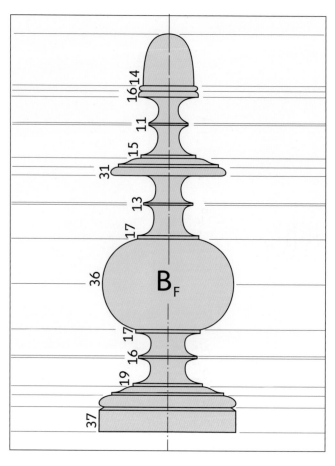

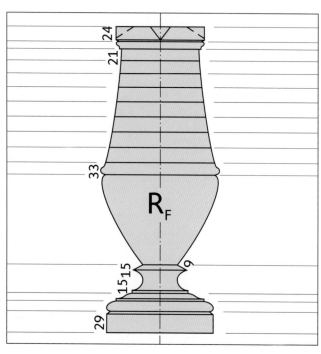

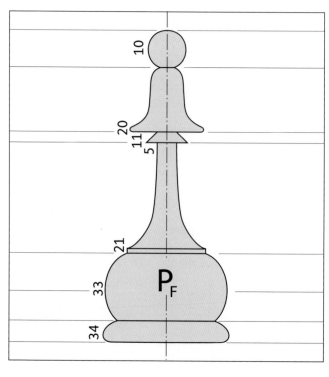

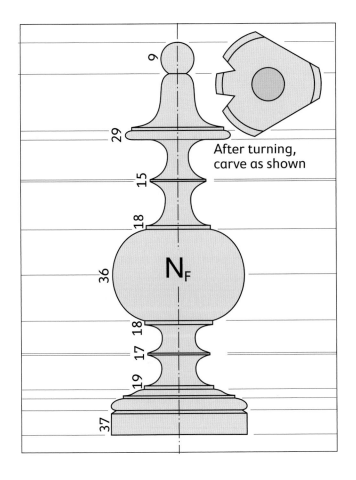

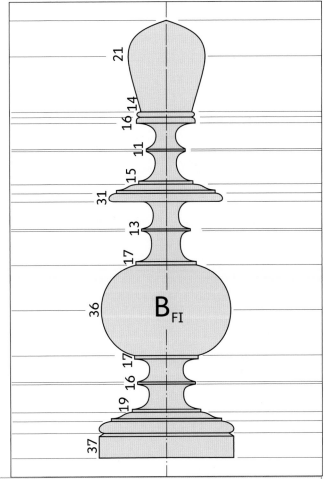

Figure 5.16 *Left and above*: pencil gauges for "improved" versions of Flinders' knight and bishop.

5.3.4 Making

The original set was turned turned between centers. As with the Rowbothum set, you could turn the men between centers (my preference), or when cantilevered from a chuck. If turning between centers you need to decide which way round the workpieces will be chucked, and whether, and if so what, waste lengths to allow.

5.4 THE WINDSOR DESIGN

Queen Elizabeth II called 1992 her *annus horribilis* because of events within her family and a serious fire at Windsor Castle. But was there an earlier fire which yielded oak from which at least one chess set was turned?

Figure 5.17 is a drawing based upon photographs of a set in the St George style shown in Gareth Williams' invaluable book on chess sets, *Master Pieces*.[16] The set's use of that style is appropriate because in discussing the set Williams states, 'In the 1820s, fire damaged the thirteenth-century church of St. George, Windsor Castle. A turner in Eton used the old oak [rescued] from the fire to make this souvenir set'. Also, on page 50 of *Master Pieces*, there's a photograph of the bottoms of two of the men showing circular paper labels which read, 'I. Parker—Eton—Turner to Her Majesty—Made from the old wood of Windsor Castle'.

In an attempt to find further details of this 1820s fire I contacted Dr Clare Rider, archivist and chapter librarian of St George's Chapel. She didn't know of any record

of a fire within the castle in the early nineteenth century, and generously wrote the following:

The description 'old wood from Windsor Castle' implies that the wood was sourced from the residential part of the Castle (i.e. the Upper Ward shown in figure 5.18) rather than from St George's Chapel in the Lower Ward—if the wood had come from St George's Chapel (figures 5.18 and 5.19) I believe this would have been specified. From 1820 to 1830, when George IV was King, he undertook extensive works on the residential and state apartments in the Upper Ward, supervised by Jeffry Wyatville and financed by a substantial Parliamentary grant. During the course of these works many of the original materials and ancient architectural features of the Castle were removed and presumably some were sold on. Some of the old wood may have subsequently come into Mr Parker's hands.

However, I notice that Mr Parker is described as 'Turner to Her Majesty', which may refer to Queen Victoria rather than the wife of a king, so it possible that he obtained the wood from renovations made in Queen Victoria's reign.

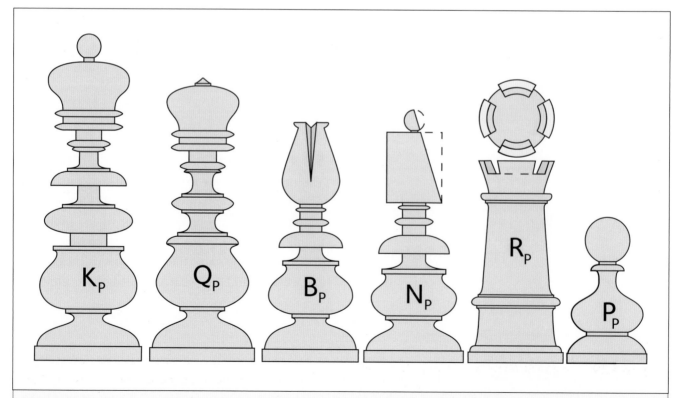

Figure 5.17 The original Parker pieces drawn from photographs in Gareth Williams' book *Master Pieces*.

Figure 5.18 An aerial view of Windsor Castle.
Sourced from Wikimedia Commons.

Figure 5.19 Inside St Georges Chapel, Windsor Castle.
Sourced from Wikimedia Commons.

(She ascended the throne on 20 June 1837.) The only major building project in the Upper Ward at this time was the reconstruction of the grand staircase to the State Apartments (figure 5.18). This had been constructed in about 1800 to replace an earlier staircase dating from the reign of King Charles II. In Victoria's reign the staircase was replaced by a new one (W St John Hope Windsor Castle I (1903) pp. 349, 369). Perhaps the wood from the old staircase was sold or given to Parker?

Whichever part of Windsor Castle the oak for Parker's set was sourced from, and why it became available, Parker's initiative illustrates the possibilities which can flow from using wood from a notable tree or other notable source and publicising that fact.

5.4.1 Design of the Parker set

Parker's original piece designs shown in figure 5.17 are attractive but somewhat confused; for example:

- Immediately below the heads of the pieces other than the rook and pawn are beads, half-beads and fillets arranged with no particular logic on shaft parts which are cylindrical or coved, again with no particular logic.

- The squat vase shapes in the king, queen, bishop and knight pieces are absent in the rook and pawn.

I therefore decided to design a version of Parker's set with clearer and more consistent signatures. I've called this design Windsor. It's shown in figures 5.20 and 5.21, and has the following features:

- Its piece signatures (which include the pieces' relative heights) are conventional.

- I decided to further clarify the queen's crown. The crowns on Parker's king and queen are both arched, but the queen's lacks an orb. However the Staunton queen's crown is unarched and pointed. Because the Staunton piece signatures are so dominant today,

I've used an unarched crown on the Windsor queen. Such crowns are typically pointed but as figure 5.22 illustrates, kings can have pointed crowns without arches. However queens can have arched crowns as figure 5.23 shows.

- I slightly increased the pawn's height to make the pawns easier to move.

- In Parker's set the heads of the bishops, knights and rooks are carved after being turned. The carving is in my view unnecessary for clear piece identification, and is therefore optional. I've omitted it from my Windsor set.

Figure 5.24 shows the Windsor set's pencil gauges.

Figure 5.20   A Windsor set turned from blackwood (*Acacia melanoxylon*) and Manchurian pear (*Pyrus ussuriensis*). The blackwood has been selected to include both heartwood and sapwood.

Figure 5.21   The Windsor pieces turned in European ash (*Fraxinus excelsior*) and blackwood (*Acacia melanoxylon*).

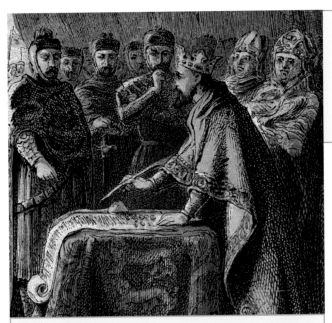

Figure 5.22   King John of England signing the Magna Carta on 15 June 1215. He is wearing a pointed crown without either arches or a cap. Two clergy wearing miters are pictures on the right.

Meaning 'great charter', the signing enshrined the rights, privileges and freedoms of the clergy and nobles (but ignored the commoners), and **>**

> thus placed limits on the power of the crown, effectively ending absolute rule.

Sourced from Wikimedia Commons, and scanned from: Kronheim, Joseph Martin. *Pictures of English History*. London: George Routledge, 1868.

Figure 5.23 The crown with arches and a velvet cap worn by Queen Consort Alexandra when she and her husband Eward VII of the United Kingdom were crowned in August 1901. Note that the arches are added to the points.

Scanned from: Fox-Davies, Arthur Charles. *A Complete Guide to Heraldry*. London: T.C. & E.C. Jack, 1909, figure 643.

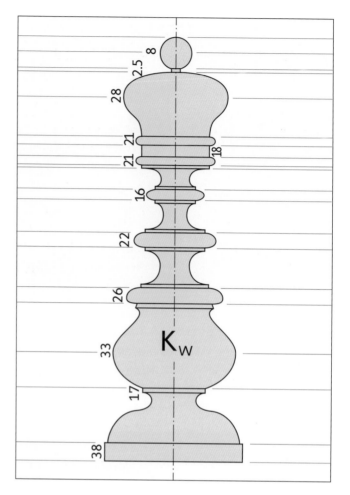

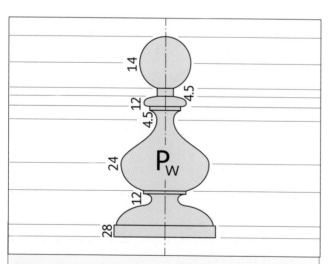

Figure 5.24 Pencil gauges for the Windsor pieces are shown in this and the following five drawings.

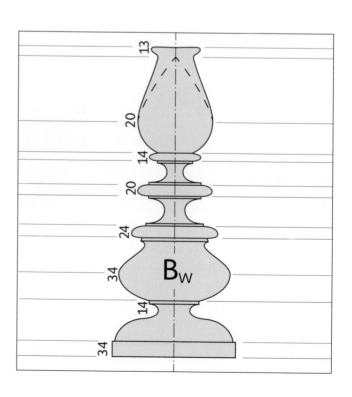

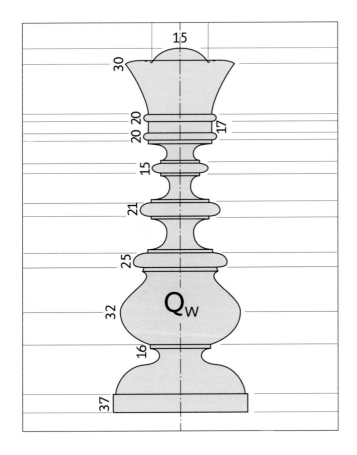

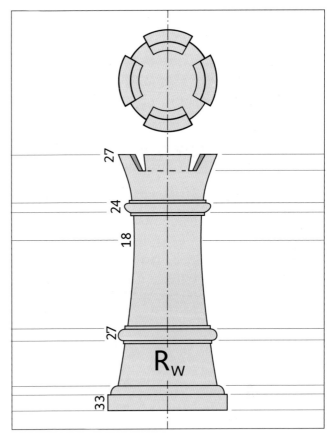

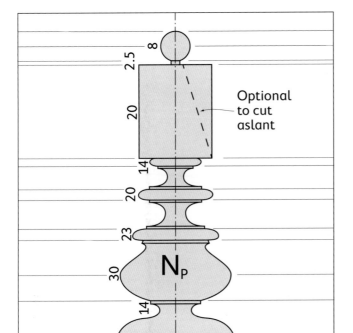

5.4.2 Making

All except the rook can be finish-turned between centers (which will require some hand carving and sanding of the tops) or when cantilevered from a scroll chuck, screwchuck, or other suitable type of chuck. Rook workpieces need to be chucked by their bottom ends so that the recess in the top can be turned.

5.5 ENDNOTES

1. Murray, H.J.R. *A History of Chess*. Oxford: Oxford University Press, 1913. p. 773.

2. Murray, H.J.R. *A History of Chess*. Oxford: Oxford University Press, 1913. p. 772.

3. Murray, H.J.R. *A History of Chess*. Oxford: Oxford University Press, 1913. p. 772

4. The Weekend Australian newspaper, January 26–27 2019, p. 3.

5. Scott, Ernest. *The Life of Matthew Flinders*. Sydney: Angus & Robertson, 2001.

6. Estensen, Miriam. *The Life of Matthew Flinders*. Crows Nest: Allen & Unwin, 2002.

7. Mundle, Rob, *Flinders the Man who Mapped Australia*. Sdney: Hatchette Australia, 2012.

8. Morgan, Kenneth. *Matthew Flinders, Maritime Explorer of Australia*. London: Bloomsbury, 2016.

9. Courtenay, Bryce. *Matthew Flinders' Cat*. Australia: Viking Publishing, 2002.

10. Trim accompanies Flinders in statues at Donington, Lincolnshire (Flinders' birthplace), and at Port Lincoln, South Australia.

11. Bernstein, William. *Masters of the Word*. London: Atlantic Books, 2013, pp. 43–47.

12. Williams, Gareth. *Master Pieces*. London: Quintet Publishing, 2000. pp. 38–39.

13. Kloprogge, Mathieu and Ine. *Chessmen Art and History*. Amsterdam: Gopher B.V., 2007, pp. 101–106.

14. Liddell, Donald M. *Chessmen*. New York: Harcourt, Crace and Company, 1937. An unnumbered plate.

15. Kloprogge, Mathieu and Ine. *Chessmen Art and History*. Amsterdam: Gopher B.V., 2007, p. 101.

16. Williams, Gareth. *Master Pieces*. London: Quintet Publishing, 2000. pp. 50–51.

Chapter 6

FIVE RECENT CHESS SET DESIGNS

This chapter first discusses some of the issues related to creating new chess set designs.

The Imagery of Chess was a group exhibition of chess sets and chess-related furniture, paintings and drawings by 32 artists which opened on 12 December 1944 at the Julien Levy Gallery in New York. It's the subject of the 2005 book *The Imagery of Chess Revisited*, edited by Larry List.[1] The book's photographs of sets by Marcel Duchamp, Man Ray and Yves Tanguy inspired me to design and make three new sets between 2012 and 2018. These are discussed before my Lopez and Stamma designs, introduced in 2004 in *Turned Chessmen*, are revisited.

6.1 CREATING NEW DESIGNS

In creating new chess set designs one's design freedom should be constricted by the desirability of high playability. I believe that if a chess player is unable to confidently identify what piece any man is when first playing with a set, that set doesn't deserve to be regarded as a chess set, and is instead a collection of small related sculptures. Many "chess sets" fail this playability test.

In the preceding chapter I defined set, side and piece signatures, and piece symbols. A clear set signature is not essential for a playing set, but reflects what Ernest Gombrich called man's desire for a sense of order.[2] However, distinctive and clear side and piece signatures and piece symbols are vital contributors to playability. Other factors are the forms and dimensions of a set's pieces because these affect stability and durability; they also determine how easy it is to move a man without disturbing its neighbors when a game is being played on a board which has squares of the optimum size.

A design which rates well in all these attributes is the Staunton shown in figure 4.1. It's named after Howard Staunton (figure 4.2). His signature appeared on the

Figure 6.1 White pieces of the Staunton design produced by the House of Staunton. The knight is nicely carved: in many sets it's not.

label in the box in which the early Staunton sets were sold. He also received a commission on sales. The set was however designed by Nathanial Cook. Its design was registered in 1849, and the set was first advertised for sale on 29 September 1849 by John Jaques & Son. This company, now called Jaques of London, continues to manufacture the Staunton design, introduced croquet into Britain, and its founder invented table tennis.

The Staunton design is mandated for tournament play so that a player can't claim that he or she was confused by the design of one or more of the men and therefore made a wrong move.

The Staunton's piece symbols are:

- an arched crown for a king (figure 6.3)

Figure 6.2   Howard Staunton (1810—1874), Shakespearean scholar and England's leading chess player and chess writer during the middle of the 19th century.

For those wishing to learn more about Staunton, the biography *Howard Staunton the English World Chess Champion* is recommended.[3]

Scanned from the *Illustrated London News*, 1874.

- a pointed crown for a queen. However as figures 6.4 (and 5.23) demonstrate, pointed crowns aren't particular to queens
- a miter for a bishop. (It's believed that the miter evolved from the Phrygian cap or frigium, a conical cap worn in the Graeco-Roman world.) A miter could also be thought of as a two-pointed crown
- a charger's head for a knight
- a castle tower for a rook
- a sphere for a pawn.

Because of the Staunton design's status and ubiquity, a set designed for today's players shouldn't conflict with the Staunton's piece symbols unless it's intended that the new design's piece symbols have a different basis or theme. Figure 6.4 shows a set whose pieces are based on the Indian army (as were the first chess sets). A more recent basis is the ways in which the different pieces are moved (see figures 1.57 and 1.67 in *Turned Chessmen*).

Because of the immense number and variety of extant designs and the desirability of ensuring playability, it's difficult to produce a new design of great freshness. Why bother to try? The French novelist and Nobel

Figure 6.3   An arched crown.

Scanned from Fox-Davies A. C. *Complete Guide to Heraldry*. London: T. C. & E. C. Jack, 1909, p. 359.

Prize for Literature winner Anatole France (1844–1924) advised, "When a thing has been said and well, have no scruple. Take it and copy it". A more recent and popular version is "God gave you eyes, so plagiarise". However most commercial 20th- and 21st-century chess set designs are copyright. Therefore if you decide to design a chess set based upon a copyrighted design, your design should be sufficiently different to avoid the risk of legal action. Even so, I suggest you still make appropriate reference to the original set and to its designer (who is ideally long dead).

Figure 6.4   A pointed crown shown in a portrait of Lothair, king of West Francia between 954 and 986 AD. This portrait, painted in 1838 by Raymond Monvoisin, is one of a series of the kings of France commissioned by Louis Philippe I. It is in the collection of the Palace of Versailles.
   Sourced from Wikimedia Commons.

6.2   THE BUENOS DESIGN

This section introduces Marcel Duchamp (figure 6.6) and the chess set he designed while in Buenos Aires (the

Figure 6.5   A set with Indian-army piece signatures used on a paved courtyard at the Jai Mahal Palace Hotel in Jaipur, Rajastan.
   Sourced from Wikimedia Commons.

Figure 6.6   Marcel Duchamp (1887–1968) in 1913.
   Sourced from Wikimedia Commons.

name means 'good airs' in Spanish); it then discusses my Buenos set design which, while retaining features of the Duchamp set, is perhaps more logical.

6.2.1 Marcel Duchamp

Frenchman Marcel Duchamp was the outstanding chess player among the dada artists. To avoid World War I Duchamp left Paris in 1915 and went to New York. After visiting Buenos Aires from New York during 1918 and 1919 Duchamp decided to concentrate on chess rather than art, and did so until the early 1930s. He unsuccessfully attempted to win the French Chess Championship, but did represent France in tournaments and Olympiads. He was awarded the title of Chess Master by the French Chess Federation, published a book on chess endgame tactics, and wrote a chess column in the Paris daily newspaper *Ce Soir*.

6.2.2 Features of Duchamp's set

Duchamp designed and was involved in making the wood chess set shown in figure 6.7 while in Buenos Aires. We don't know the details of his design objectives, nor of any restraints on the set's design and creation. However Duchamp wasn't averse to controversy, and my thoughts below on Duchamp's piece designs may reflect his intentions:

- The set signature in the king, queen, bishop and pawn is a downward-pointing trumpet with a flared top. This signature is entirely absent from the knight, and is modified in the rook and the pawn.

- The king and queen are the same height—in most sets kings are typically noticeably taller than queens.

- Duchamp's king's piece signature is a pointed crown, the queen's may represent an arched crown. In the ubiquitous Staunton design the king has the arched crown, the queen the pointed crown.

- Below the king's crown are four adjacent rings. There are three rings below the queen's crown, but they are separated by narrow fillets. Then the bishop has one ring, not two as you might expect. The rook and pawn have none. The Staunton king, queen and bishop each have three rings immediately below their piece symbols, with the upper two separated by a fillet (see figure 6.1). These rings are absent from the other three Staunton pieces.

- The knight resembles an elaborately and well-carved ram's head, not the typical charger's head, although the back of Duchamp's knight has the braided mane seen on dressage horses. Duchamp's knight is also stylistically unrelated to the set's other five pieces, and has an alien attached metal base.

Figure 6.7 The pieces of Marcel Duchamp's set designed in Buenas Aires. The battlemented top part of the rook is square in plan.

- The battlement of the rook is square in plan whereas in most, but not all, sets it is circular in plan. Several rooks each with a square battlement are shown in *Chess Masterpieces*.[4]

- the trumpet doesn't flare out under the head of the pawn as it does in the other pieces.

6.2.3 Design of the Buenos set

The set shown in figure 6.8 is my attempt to design a set which preserves many of the features of Duchamp's original design while eliminating its confusing aspects explained above. I have named my set design *Buenos*. Its features are:

- The king is the tallest piece, and the other piece heights grade down to the pawn

- Its king's and queen's crowns conform to the Staunton precedent.

- Both crowns would have more logically had two separated rings to represent the crown's band as seen in figure 6.3. However I've retained Duchamp's king's four adjacent rings, moved his queen's rings together, used two rings beneath the bishop's miter and one

which is trimmed to form the peak of the knights helmet. There are other patterns of rings which are just as logical.

- How to redesign the knight? Being a competent woodturner, but a poor wood carver, I wanted to design a turnable knight piece signature. Duchamp was French, and I thought it desirable to use a piece symbol with a French association. A representation of a tricorn hat was sometimes used (see figure 5.14), but wouldn't be familiar to most chess players today. Instead I chose a chevalier's helmet and carved some of the ring away to represent the helmet's peak.

- Duchamp's rook is striking and not confusing. I've replaced the original straight sides to the lower section of the tower by the trumpet with the flared top set signature.

- The bottom part of the pawn is flared at the top, and thus all six pieces share the same set signature.

- The pencil gauges for the Buenos design are shown in figure 6.9.

Figure 6.8   My Duchamp-inspired Buenos pieces turned in blackwood (*Acacia melanoxylon*) and tree of heaven (*Ailanthus altissima*).

Figure 6.9 The six pencil gauges for the Buenos pieces are shown below. Although leading holes aren't shown, the men of the Buenos set could be leaded.

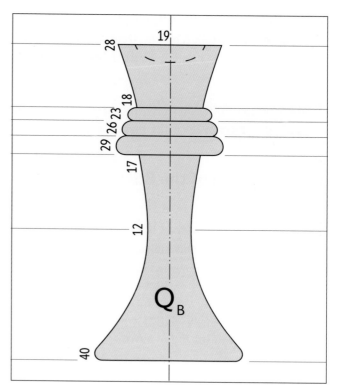

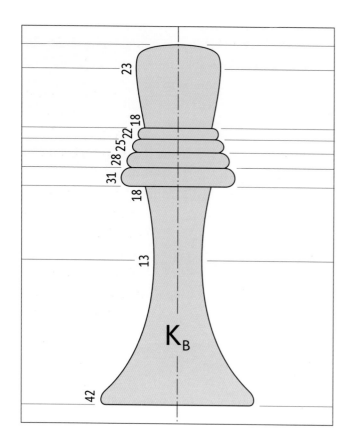

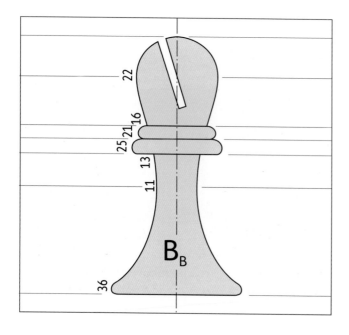

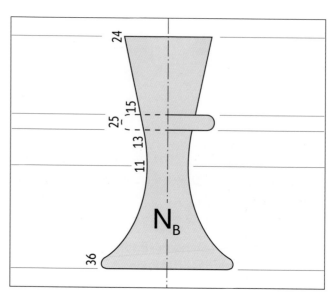

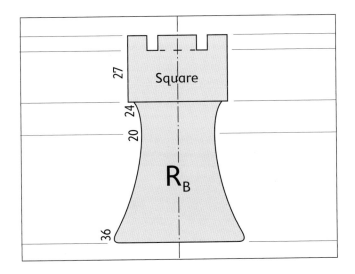

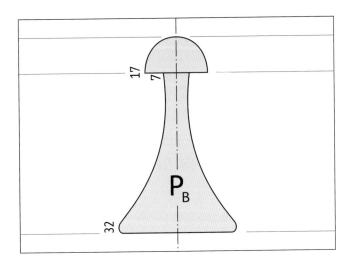

6.2.4 Making the Buenos set

I decided not to lead my Buenos set, and to finish-turn all the men on a typical turners' screwchuck, not that shown in figure 4.1. To enable this for the kings, queens, knights and pawns:

1. Prepare each workpiece by turning it between centers to a cylinder with the appropriate chucking detail at what will be its top end.
2. Chuck each workpiece by its top end, cut its bottom surface at the right-hand end very slightly concave with a skew's long point, round the edge around the bottom surface, bore the hole for the screwchuck's screw, and sand the finished bottom surface and adjacent rounded edge.
3. Mount each workpiece on the screwchuck.

4. Finish-turn the body and piece symbol.

Three pieces required further attention:

- After preparing each bishop workpiece as in steps 1 to 3 above, saw the slot in the miter piece symbol using the jig shown in figure 6.10 before finish-turning.

- For the knights, after step 4 carve most of the ring away to leave the helmet's peak, and sand.

- For each rook, its workpiece was prepared as in steps 1 to 3 except that the cylindrical workpiece's diameter had to be turned to mate with the hole in the sawing jig shown in figures 6.11 and 6.12. In my case that diameter was 1 3/4" (44.5 mm) because I had a drill of that size. The workpiece was also turned to its finished length and its top surface turned flat and sanded while chucked as in step 3. Using a table saw, I then sawed the four shallow and four deep slots as shown in figures 6.11 and 6.12. Each rook workpiece was then rechucked on the screwchuck so that the trumpet-shaped body and recess in the center of the top could be finish-turned.

The men of a Buenos set can be polished in the lathe while chucked on, or after being rechucked on, the screwchuck. If the screwchucking hole is to be filled and the bottom surface polished, this has to be done separately. Alternatively the men could be leathered.

Figure 6.10 Sawing a split in a bishop workpiece, here mounted on a screwchuck.

Figure 6.11   A sawing jig for the Buenos rooks. The jig is used to make in the top of each rook workpiece: four shallow cuts for the embrasures, and four deep cuts for each battlement's outside faces. The saw's guard has to be temporarily removed to make these cuts, so you need to take great care.

The height of the jig's body is equal to the height of a rook (56 mm). The jig has two pencil lines drawn at right angles on its top surface. These two lines must pass through the centers of the workpiece bottoms.

It's best to saw the shallow slots into all the rooks first. To do this:

1. Set the blade to the correct height (4 mm) and adjust the fence's distance from the blade so that the slots will be cut in the correct places.
2. Clamp the workpiece upside down into the jig, ideally with the annular rings parallel or at right-angles to the saw's fence. Mark on the workpiece's bottom short pencil lines which align with the pencil lines on the jig.
3. Saw the first slot as shown in figure 6.12. It's best to cut each slot with a single forward push. If you use a forward push and a backward pull to cut a groove, the backward pull can leave burning marks on the slot's surfaces.
4. Unclamp the workpiece, axially rotate the workpiece 90°, reclamp, and saw the second slot.
5. Repeat for the other two shallow slots in the workpiece. Then cut all the shallow slots in all the other rooks in the same way. **>**

> 6. Adjust the blade height (20 mm minimum) and fence distance to cut the deeper slots.
> 7. Cut all the deeper slots in all the rooks as described in steps 2 to 5 above.

Figure 6.12   Sawing a slot, here a deeper one.

6.3   THE MANNY SET

This section introduces Man Ray, discusses the chess sets he designed, and then explains the design and making of my Manny chess set.

6.3.1   Man Ray

Emmanuel Radnitzky (figure 6.13) was born in 1890 in Philadelphia to Russian Jewish parents. The family moved to Brooklyn, New York, in 1897. At the instigation of Emmanuel's brother the family changed its surname to Ray in 1935. Then, because Emmanuel was usually called Manny, he adopted the name Man Ray. He moved to Paris in 1920 and lived there until his death in 1976, apart from the war years 1940 to 1951 spent back in the United States.

Ray was a major Dada and Surrealist artist who worked in many media especially photography. He was also a keen chess player (he often played with Marcel Duchamp), and between 1920 and 1962 an active chess set designer. His sets were manufactured in small batches in wood and in metals including aluminium and silver.

In 2013 an authorised replica in silver of a Man Ray set made £26,000 at auction.

Much of the above information was sourced from the biography *Man Ray* by Arturo Schwarz.[5]

Figure 6.13 Man Ray right with Salvador Dali photographed in 1934.
Sourced from Wikimedia Commons.

6.3.2 Features of Man Ray's Pieces

Figure 6.14 shows the forms of some of Man Ray's pieces from different sets. In Ray's set designs:

- Early kings were tall, four-sided pyramids representing the tombs of early Egyptian kings or pharaohs.

- Queens were tall cones representing wimples. These medieval headdresses were worn by wealthy women. Ray added orbs in later versions—an orb is a common queen piece symbol.

- Early bishops were often in the form of flagons because of the clergy's associations with liqueurs and spirits. Later bishop piece symbols were miters.

- Knights move in a dog-leg. In Ray's first set he represented this by the scrolls of scrap violins. Later knights achieved similar but simpler forms by being segments cut from specially profiled rings.

- Ray's early rooks were cubes. Later rooks more closely resembled castle towers, and featured slots to represent embrasures.

- Ray's early pawns were relatively massive reflecting Ray's opinion that conventional pawn designs downplayed the real power of pawns in play.

Figure 6.14 The forms of some Man Ray pieces turned in blackwood (*Acacia melanoxylon*). *Left to right*: a king in the form of a pyramid, a queen represented by a wimple-resembling cone, a flask-shaped bishop, a cubic rook, and a pawn which is larger relative to the other pieces than is typical.

- Ray's kings and queens had equal heights, as had his pawns and rooks in some sets. A particular feature of the Staunton and most chess set designs is that different pieces have different heights. In particular the king is taller than the queen and the pawn is shorter and also less massive than the other five pieces.

6.3.1 Design of the Manny pieces

A design reflects both its designer's objectives and the constraints which the designer willingly accepts or is forced to accept. As explained on page 43, when I design a chess set I believe that a chess-playing stranger should be able to use that set without needing to have the piece signatures explained. And being a woodturner of acceptable standard but an indifferent woodcarver, I usually design all my sets' pieces to be fully turned, or, if not, to have minimal carving—the appearance of many sets is spoiled by crudely carved knights.

My intention with the Manny pieces shown in figure 6.15 was to echo some features of Ray's piece designs while increasing playability by having a more consistent set signature and piece signatures which conform more closely to Staunton's. I decided to size my set design for a board with 50 mm x 50 mm squares.

Conical lower sections are a feature of some of Ray's

piece designs and are found in many other sets; for example, Peter Toepfer's shown in figure 6.40. I adopted the cone as the Manny set's set signature, and it is present in all six pieces.

Features of the Manny piece signatures shown in figure 6.16 are:

- The king has a stylised arched crown following the Staunton precedent.

- The queen has an orb surmounting the cone.

- The knight follows Ray's use of a section cut from a turned and profiled ring. The Manny ring's cross section is however different, and repeats the conical set signature.

- Piece heights conform to the Staunton norm and don't follow Ray's equal-height kings and queens.

- The Manny pawns are the smallest men, unlike those in the Ray-designed sets.

The pencil gauges for the Manny pieces except the knight are shown in figure 6.16.

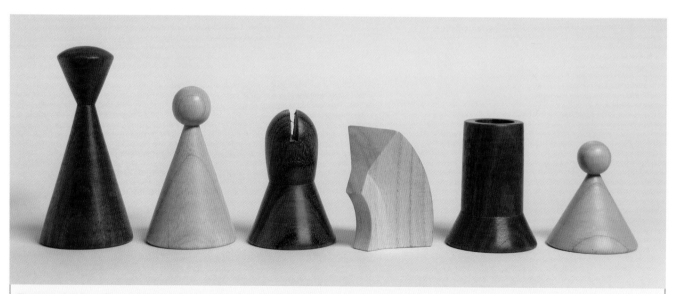

Figure 6.15 The pieces of the Manny set turned in blackwood (*Acacia melanoxylon*) and Manchurian pear (*Pyrus ussuriensis*).

Figure 6.16 Pencil gauges for five of the Manny pieces. Leading holes are shown, but leading is optional. The pencil gauge/design for the Manny knight is shown later in the making part of this section.

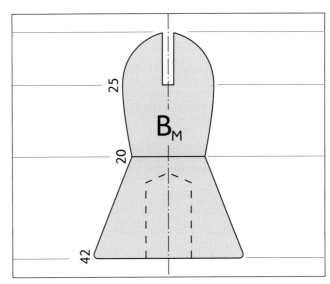

B_M

25

20

42

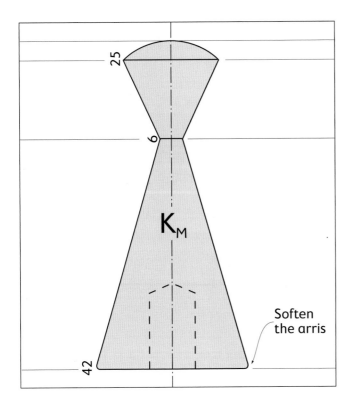

K_M

25

6

42

Soften the arris

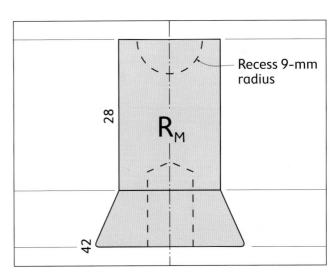

R_M

Recess 9-mm radius

28

42

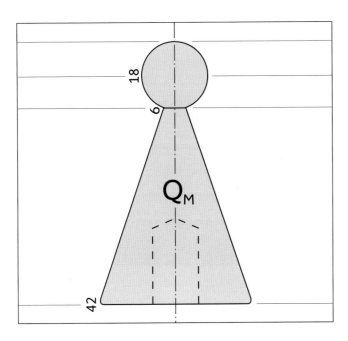

Q_M

18

6

42

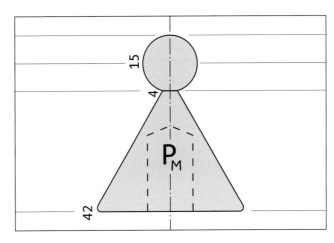

P_M

15

4

42

6.3.2   Making the Manny pieces

This subsection will first outline making the men except the knights, and then explain making the knights.

Making the five non-knight pieces

If you're leading your Manny set or finish-turning them on a conventional screwchuck, prepare, and bore your men's workpieces using the methods shown in figures 4.5 to 4.10.

The slot in the bishop's miter can be sawn as shown in figure 6.10, but with the top surface of the jig being horizontal, and positioned at half the saw kerf's width below lathe-axis height. Alternatively use a jig similar to that shown in figure 6.17 with a table saw.

The workpieces are than chucked for finish-turning, and ideally subsequently rechucked for polishing.

Figure 6.17   Sawing the miter slot in a bishop workpiece before finish-turning. The cylindrical workpiece is clamped into the vee sawn into the body of the jig.

Making the knights

The knight is the most demanding Manny piece to make. Its design is shown in figure 6.18. The steps in making a set's knights are.

1. Prepare two workpieces, one for the black side's knights, and one for the white side's knights. Each

workpiece should be a disk with transverse grain slightly oversize in thickness and diameter; that is more than 100 mm in diameter, and more than 32-mm thick.

2. Drill a hole (typically between 6- and 7-mm diameter) through the center of each disk. Use the hole to mount one of the disks on a screwchuck.

3. If the left-hand face of the disk which is being pulled against the right-hand face of the screwchuck isn't flat, turn the right-hand face of the disk flat and rechuck the disk on the screwchuck with the just-flatted disk face against the right-hand face of the screwchuck.

4. Finish-turn the disk's periphery to 100-mm diameter. Finish-turn the disk's right-hand face so that the width of the periphery is 32 mm. Only turn the central 40-mm-diameter recess to a depth of about 5 mm as shown in figure 6.19. Sand the finish-turned surfaces.

5. Repeat steps 3 and 4 for the second workpiece.

6. Prepare a backing plate about 120-mm in diameter—I used 19-mm-thick plywood for it. Drill a central hole and mount it on a screwchuck. True its periphery and pencil circles of 40-mm- and 100-mm-diameter on its right-hand face.

7. Dechuck the backing plate. Draw on what was its right-hand face where you'll later make the saw cuts to free the two knights from each disk workpiece.

8. Drill three holes (shown in figures 6.18 to 6.20) through the backing disk for screwing the workpiece onto the backing disk.

9. Remount the backing disk on the screwchuck with the face with the pencil lines drawn in step 7 above against the right-hand face of the screwchuck.

10. Compare the outside diameters of the two workpiece peripheries adjacent to their finish-turned faces. Select the workpiece whose diameter is smallest.

11. Draw a circle of 100-mm diameter on the right-hand face of the backing plate. Turn a small annular recess

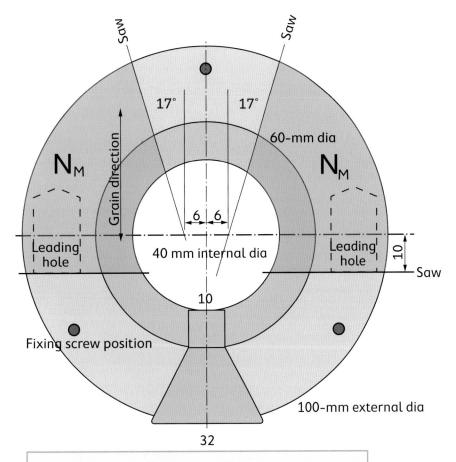

Figure 6.18 The design of the Manny workpiece disk showing how it yields two knights.

Figure 6.19 Screwchuck, backing plate, and a Manny workpiece for two knights. The upper face and periphery of the workpiece has been finish-turned and sanded, and had been chucked (including being screwed) into the annular recess in the underside of the backing plate before being dechucked for this photograph.

Figure 6.20 About to screw the backing plate and workpiece assembly onto the screwchuck for finish-turning the other face of the workpiece.

in the backing plate's right-hand face so that the outer edge of the finish-turned face of the selected workpiece locates snuggly.

12. Screw the workpiece into and against the backing plate. Ensure that the screws are not so long that they will be hit when finish-turning the right-hand face of the workpiece.

13. Finish-turn the right-hand face of the workpiece. Cut the perimeter of the central 40-mm-diameter recess all the way through so as to leave a 40-mm diameter through hole.

14. Dechuck the backing plake and workpiece assembly, but don't undo the three screws.

15. Saw along the waste side of the lines to free the two knights. Only saw just past the 40-mm pencil circle. This enables the same backing plate to be reused to turn the other side's pair of knights.

16. Screw the backing plate back onto the screwchuck as it was earlier. If necessary widen the annular recess so that the outer edge of the finished face of the second workpiece locates snuggly.

17. Repeat steps 12 to 15 for the second workpiece.

18. Sand the sawn faces of the knights by rubbing those faces on abrasive paper or cloth supported on a flat surface.

19. I drilled each leading hole by hand using a hand brace and a 1/2"-diameter auger. For this I held each knight in a padded vice.

20. Polish the knights.

Figure 6.22   Making the first of the four bandsaw cuts needed to free the two knights.

Figure 6.21   Finish-turning the second face of the workpiece with a 12-mm-wide detail gouge.

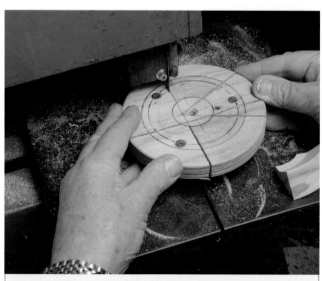

Figure 6.23   Making a second bandsaw cut.

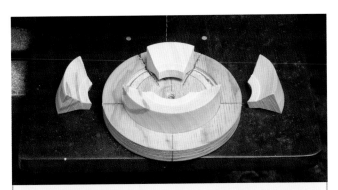

Figure 6.24 Bandsawing completed, and the assemblage shown in the preceding two figures turned over. The two Manny knights have been sawn free while the two waste pieces remain screwed to the backing plate.

6.4   THE TANG DESIGN

In this section I'll discuss my Tang design, a set design based on the cylinder—for a competent woodturner almost the antithesis of craftsmanship. However the challenge of the cylindrical design constraint can be overcome to yield sets which are elegant, fresh, and have high playability. This cylindrical constraint was notably challenged and overcome by Raymond Georges Yves Tanguy, known as Yves Tanguy, who in the The Imagery of Chess exhibition showed a set sawn from dowel or possibly from a broom handle with the men painted black or white according to side.[6] A cylinder-based set inspired by Tanguy's set but with its sides painted respectively orange and purple is pictured in *Master Pieces*.[7]

6.4.1   Features of the Tang design

My design shown in figure 6.25 is clearly inspired by Tanguy's, and I hence call its design *Tang*. (The Chinese dynasty which began in 618 and lasted until 907 AD is also called *Tang*.) However the Tang design, including the five knight variants, shown in figures 6.25 and 6.26 has piece signatures which differ considerably from and are at least as definitive as Tanguy's set: it also assumes that the maker has a lathe whereas Tanguy's pieces were made by appropriately sawing through a dowel or broom handle (although the sawn surfaces were later sanded smooth).

Figure 6.25 The Tang design with the Jorn-Pfab-inspired knight. Rather than seek to obscure that the set is made from wood as Tanguy did, the dark heartwood of blackwood (*Acacia melanoxylon*) is used for the men of the black side, the men of the white side show both blackwood sapwood and heartwood.

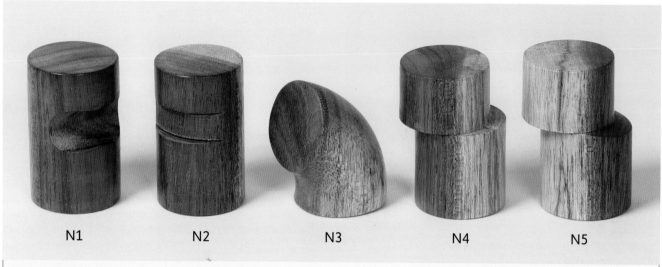

Figure 6.26   Five options for Tang knights.

The Tang design's features are:

- The piece heights reduce steadily from king to pawn. (Tanguy's rook is taller than both his knight and pawn.)

- In the Staunton set shown in figure 6.1 the top part of the king represents an arched crown, and the top part of the queen a crown with points and without arches. These two types of crown are represented by the convex and concave tops of the Tang's king and queen respectively.

- The bishop has a vertical slot or channel which represents the gap between the front and back parts of a miter.

- Relatively shorter than Tanguy's original, the Tang's rook has a turned recess in its top which creates the impression of a tower with a battlement—this is optional, but aids piece identification. I haven't bothered to cut slots to represent embrasures.

- To represent the knight's dog-leg move, Tanguy cleverly sawed the top and bottom surfaces of his knight parallel but not at a right angle to the cylinder's longitudinal axis so that the piece's side elevation was a rhombus.

- Figure 6.26 shows five alternative turned knight pieces.

  i)   The drilled hole in knight N1, a feature introduced by Jorn Pfab, results in a piece signature which might represent a charger's head and neck, or a *sight*, the gap in a knight's helmet which in some types of helmet was covered by a visor?

  ii) By turning knight N2 on two parallel axes, a more convincing sight can be created. Adding eyes in the bottom of the sight, as in the set designed and made by New South Wales turner Ernie Newman and his son (*Turned Chessmen*, page 67) is optional.

  iii) Knight N3 is cut from a ring with a circular cross section.

  iv) A knight's dog-leg move is recalled by knights N4 and N5. The vertical axes of their two cylinders are displaced from the other by 5 mm (approximately a sixth of the diameter of the two cylinders), and the heights of the two cylinders are in the ratio 3:2.

- Tanguy's pawn is a cylinder which has the same diameter as the other pieces, but is unusually short being only a quarter of the height of the king. On a board whose squares' side length is little more than the diameter of the pieces, it could be difficult to move a pawn without displacing other chessmen. The cylindrical finials of the Tang pawns make them easier to access and move.

I designed my Tang pieces pictured for a board with 43 x 43 mm squares, and chose 28 mm (65% of 43 mm) as the cylinder diameter. Because of the need to grip men to lift, move and place them, this cylinder diameter should decrease as a percentage of the board square's breadth the further that breadth is below 43 mm. Similarly, that percentage can be increased as the board square's breadth increases above 43 mm.

Figure 6.27 shows the pencil gauges for all the Tang pieces except the knights. The designs of the five Tang knight variants are shown in figures 6.28 to 6.32.

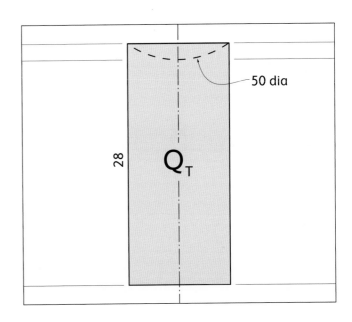

50 dia

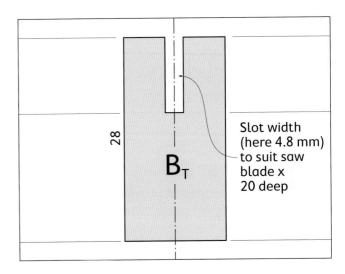

Slot width (here 4.8 mm) to suit saw blade x 20 deep

Figure 6.27 The five pencil gauges below are for the Tang queen, king, bishop, rook, and pawn. The Tang men could be leaded, but a different method would be needed for the pawns. Sharp arrises should be appropriately softened.

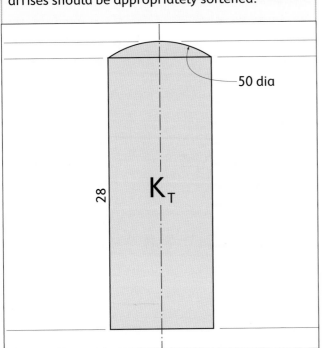

50 dia

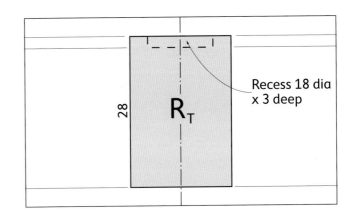

Recess 18 dia x 3 deep

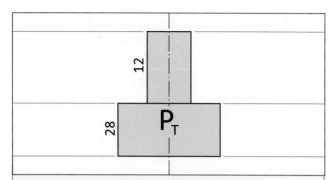

Figure 6.27 continued   The pencil gauge for the Tang pawn.

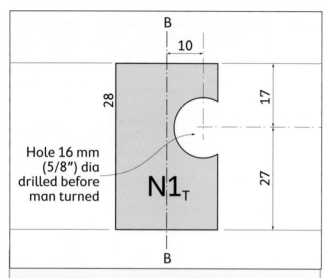

Figure 6.28   The pencil gauge for Tang knight N1.

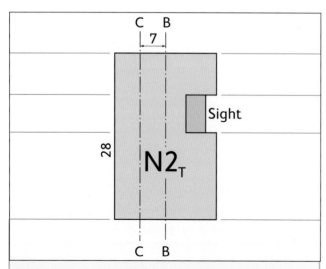

Figure 6.29   The pencil gauge for Tang knight N2.

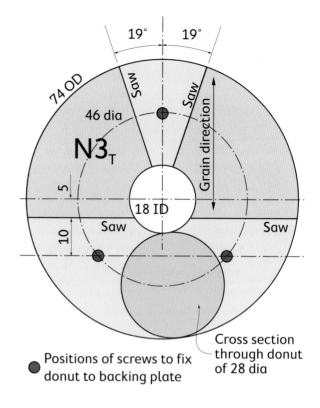

Figure 6.30   The pencil gauge for Tang knight N3.

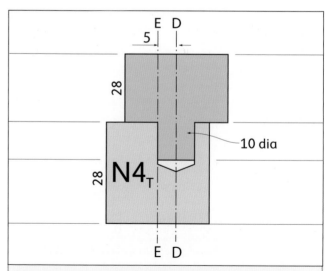

Figure 6.31   The pencil gauge for Tang knight N4. It's turned in two parts which are glued together. Take care that the grain in the two parts aligns.

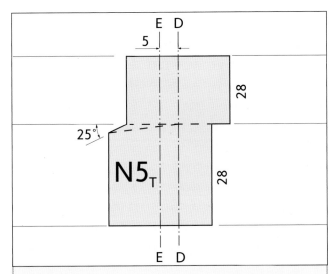

Figure 6.32 The pencil gauge for Tang knight N5. The workpiece is first turned on one axis, then the other.

Screw through the backing plate to hold the transposed workpiece into the recess. Finish-turn the remaining quarter of the periphery. The two men are then sawn free as shown in figures 6.22 to 6.24, and their sawn ends sanded prior to polishing.

- **Knight N4** This knight piece is in two separate parts which are glued together. Ideally the grain in the two parts should align so that it appears that each knight is turned in one piece on two axes.

- **Knight N5** This knight is turned in one piece either wholly between centers on two parallel axes, or as shown in figures 6.33 to 6.39 on the same two axes first between centers and then cantilevered from a scroll chuck.

6.4.2 Making

Making the Tang pieces except the knights is straightforward. When preparing workpieces allow waste appropriate to the chucking sequence and methods used.

Making the Tang knights
How to turn the different knights is explained below:

- **Knight N1** Prepare a workpiece with a rectangular cross section, bore the hole, then finish-turn with the workpiece mounted along axis B–B.

- **Knight N2** Finish-turn the body with the workpiece mounted along axis B–B. Remount the workpiece along axis C–C, and turn the sight slot. To do so cut down its two sides with canted V-cuts ahead of using a parting tool then a narrow skew to cut the sight's bottom.

- **Knight N3** The workpiece for a side's pair of knights is a transverse-grained disk. Mount the disk on a screwchuck, and finish-turn three quarters of its surface. Prepare a backing plate held on a screwchuck. Turn into it a shallow annular recess whose diameter at its center is 46 mm. Drill the three holes through the backing plate shown in figure 6.30.

Figure 6.33 The workpiece mounted along axis D–D, roughed to about 40-mm diameter, and marked out from the pencil gauge. Allow at least a 5-mm length of waste at the right-hand end so that the recess left by the tail center won't be left in the top of the finished knight. At least a 25-mm length of waste should be left at the left-hand end to allow for the chucking spigot (here already turned) and parting-off.

Figure 6.34 The right-hand end of the right-hand part of the knight has been turned to 28-mm diameter, and its right-hand end marked with a V-cut. In the center of the workpiece a series of canted V-cuts has been taken down to 28-mm diameter. In this series of cuts the right-hand face is flat and vertical, and the left hand face slopes at 25° (the sharpening angle of my skew).

Figure 6.35 I've used a series of canted V-cuts taken down to about 20-mm diameter to define the bottom surface of the knight.

Figure 6.36 The workpiece has been remounted along axis E–E, and the left-hand end of the lower part has been turned to about 29 mm diameter with a parting tool.

Figure 6.37 The right-hand end of the lower part of the knight has been roughed so that its perimeter is close to the apparent diameter of the knight's right-hand part.

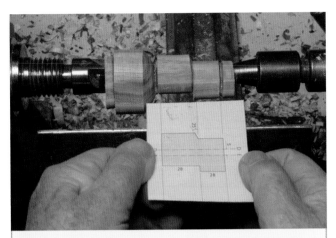

Figure 6.38 Using careful canted V-cuts I've finish-turned the flat underside of the knight's top part, then finish-turned, including sanding, the cylindrical surface of the knight's bottom part.

Figure 6.39 The workpice is now cantilevered from a scroll chuck along axis D–D. The top of the knight's top part has been finish-turned as has the top part's cylindrical surface. The knight is being parted off at its left-hand end, again using canted V-cuts.

6.5 THE LOPEZ DESIGN

Some of Man Ray's chessmen had plain conical bodies as figure 6.14 illustrates. However Peter Toepfer earlier designed the set shown in figure 6.40 in which all the men's bodies were cones. In 2003 I decided to design a set which was fully turned, easy to turn, and have piece signatures which would be readily recognised by players familiar with those of the Staunton design. I decided that the design would have conical piece signatures, and called it Lopez.

The Lopez design was introduced on pages 65 and 115 of *Turned Chessmen* and is shown in figure 6.41 below. I named it after Ruy López, a Spanish priest and author of the chess text *Libro de la invencion liberal y arte del juego del Axedrez*, published in Alcala, Spain 1n 1561. This text consisted of ninety-five chapters spread

Figure 6.40 Mr Peter Toepfer's patented exhibition chessmen. The bodies are aluminium cones which nest, and the piece symbols detach so that the whole set packs into one trunk for transport. The cloth board's black and white squares are 762 mm square.

Peter G. Toepfer (1857–1915) was a chess enthusiast fromm Milwaukee, Wisconsin. Information about this set is scanty, and the chessmen seem to have disappeared. Toepfer was teaching with this set between 1900 and 1904.

Sourced from: Wilson, Fred, editor, *A Picture History of Chess*. New York: Dover Publications, 1981, p. 70, and www.cs1904.com/lost sets. htm. Also previously shown on page 90 of *Turned Chessmen*.

Figure 6.41   A Lopez set. The conical bases are turned from southern silky oak, *Grevillea robusta*. The piece symbols are turned from London plane, *Platanus acerifolia,* and black apple, *Planchonella australis*.

through four books. An Italian translation was published in Venice in 1584. A game opening described in the book, now called the Ruy Lopez or Spanish opening is one of the most popular in chess.[8]

6.5.1   Design

The major problem was designing a knight which retained the conical set signature, had a Staunton-conforming charger's head and neck piece symbol, and yet was fully turned. Tilting the conical body proved to be the key.

Pencil gauges for the Lopez pieces are shown in figure 6.42 and in figure 6.43. All gauges show pieces in two parts. Depending on how you decide to differentiate the two sides, you could instead turn all except the knights in one piece.

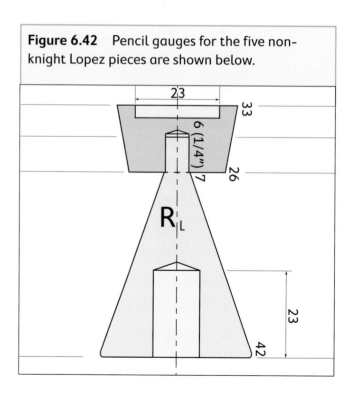

Figure 6.42   Pencil gauges for the five non-knight Lopez pieces are shown below.

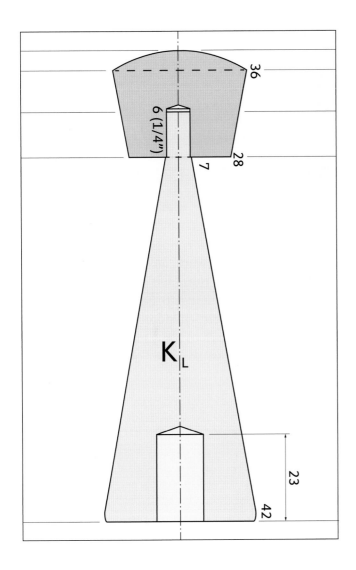

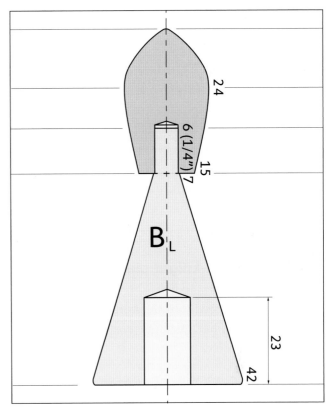

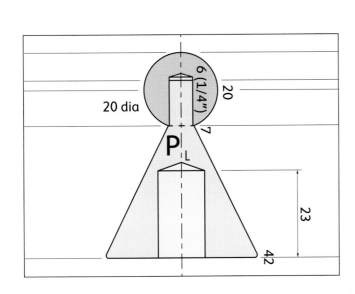

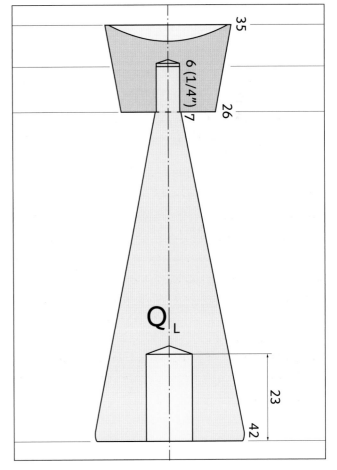

6.5.2   Making the Lopez pieces

Because it is easy to turn and requires almost no carving, the Lopez design has indeed proved a popular project for woodturners. How to make the five Lopez pieces except the knight is explained first. Instructions to make a knight follow. I've assumed that the set will be leaded, and that all men have separate piece symbols.

As usual, before starting, think through and decide exactly how you'll make the different pieces. How you'll polish may influence these decisions, and will often cause you to delay parting off as long as possible.

Making the non-knight pieces

After the bottom of a body has been finish-turned and the leading hole bored with the workpiece cantilevered from a chuck, to finish-turn the remainder of the body and its pin you could:

- continue turning with the workpiece cantilevered from the chuck. The risk of the pin snapping is then high

- eliminate the risk of the pin snapping by mounting a live center with a conical nose in the tailstock, and locating the conical nose into the mouth of the leading hole. As you turn the men of a set, this method necessitates continually swapping between the live center and the drill which is held in a Jacobs chuck or has a Morse taper.

- remove the workpiece from the chuck and turn it between between centers.

- rechuck the workpiece by its leading hole using a chuck such as shown in figures 4.1 to 4.4. This would necessitate choosing a compatible diameter for the leading hole.

Making the separate piece symbols for the non-knights is shown in figures 6.43 to 6.47.

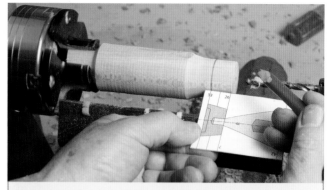

Figure 6.43   Turning a white side's rook's piece symbol. Several piece symbols can be turned from a cantilevered workpiece about 150 mm long. Here I've flattened and sanded the workpiece's right-hand end, bored the 6-mm (1/4")-diameter hole, calipered the right-hand end of the workpiece to the 33-mm diameter at the top of the symbol, and have marked the symbol's height.

Figure 6.44   Checking the diameter at the bottom of the rook's piece symbol.

Figure 6.45 Parting off the white rook's piece symbol. I've allowed about a 1 mm thickness of waste so that after rechucking the top of the symbol can be finish-turned to leave a clean surface.

Figure 6.46 About to chuck the rook piece symbol on a pin turned in waste wood. The fit needs to be tight to allow the top of the symbol to be gently finish-turned.

Figure 6.47 Gently shear-scraping the recess in the top of the rook's piece symbol.

Making the knight bodies

The figure 6.48 pencil gauge illustrates that the knight bodies are turned first on axis A–A, then on axis A–B. The head is turned separately on axis C–C.

The sequence to make a knight's body is shown in figures 6.49 to 6.55.

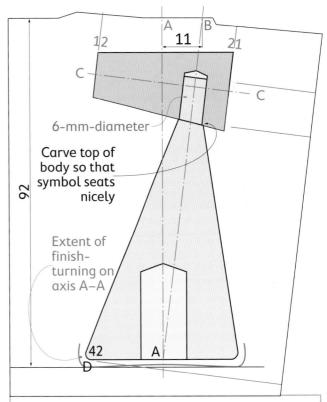

Figure 6.48 Pencil gauge for the Lopez knight.

Figure 6.49   Two Lopez knight workpieces marked out ready for turning. A face and an edge have been dressed at right angles to each other, the workpieces have been sawn to 92-mm long, and the centers A and B marked out from the two dressed surfaces.

Figure 6.51   Boring the leading hole. The blue tape ia a depth gauge.

Before boring, I trimmed the workpiece's right-hand end back 2 mm and cut it slightly concave with a skew's long point. I then finishe-turned the area defined by the blue curve at the bottom of figure 6.48.

Figure 6.50   While mounted between centers along axis A–A, the workpiece has been roughed to cylinder, had a chucking spigot turned at one end, and been chucked by that spigot.

The figure 6.48 pencil gauge assumes that 2 mm will be trimmed from the right-hand end—hence the pencil line at the right-hand end of this workpiece. A 42-mm diameter area has been turned towards the workpiece's right-hand end with a parting tool to enable the workpiece's right-hand end to be finish-turned.

Figure 6.52   After the finish-turning and boring described in figure 6.51 have been completed, I mounted the workpiece along axis A–B between a pronged drive center and a live center with a conical nose. If you don't have a suitable tail center, you could turn a plug which fits in the leading hole and onto the nose of your tail center.

Figure 6.53 Marking out the junction between the body and the pin from the two red lines on the right-hand edge of the figure 6.48 pencil gauge. The right-hand red line should be square to the lathe axis and align with the extreme right of the workpiece (point D in figure 6.48).

Figure 6.54 Starting to plane the body. I have parted the pin to about 10-mm diameter rather than to its final diameter so that there's no risk of snapping it.

Figure 6.55 Planing the body. I have parted the pin to its finished 6-mm diameter, and am planing less vigorously than in the preceding figure.

Making the knight piece symbols

The charger's head cone frustrums are turned and parted off much as shown in figures 6.43 to 6.45. How I held the frustrums for drilling is shown in figure 6.56.

When gluing the charger's head onto the pin you'll need to slightly trim the top of the body to achieve a neat fit.

Figure 6.56 Drilling a charger's head. It's clamped by being tapped between the two pieces of wood screwed to the plywood. The farther piece is fixed in position using two screws. The nearer piece is held by a single, central screw, and thus can pivot. Have the symbol's annual rings horizontal or vertical when it's drilled.

The blue tape on the drill is a depth gauge.

6.6   THE STAMMA DESIGN

A turner from Kearney, Nebraska, asked me to produce working drawings for the pieces of my Stamma chess set design pictured on page 66 of *Turned Chessmen*. The design's version shown in figure 6.57 is slightly squatter than that pictured in *Turned Chessmen*, and I haven't sawn or carved an optional slit in the bishop's miter.

Phillip Stamma (c. 1705–c. 1755) was born in Aleppo in what is now Syria. He became a professional chess player, moved to Paris, and there in 1737 self-published a book of a hundred studies of chess problems entitled *Essai sur le Jeu des Échecs*. The book is dedicated to Lord Harrington, then Secretary of State for the Britain's Northern Department. Harrington responded by in 1739 appointing Stamma as Interpreter of Oriental Languages to the British Government at a salary of £80 a year.

Stamma therefore moved to London. There in 1745 he self-published *The Noble Game of Chess*. This translation and revision of his earlier book also included an additional seventy-four lines of analysis of opening moves.

Stamma frequented Old Slaughter's coffee house shown in figure 6.58. There in 1747 he played ten games against Francois-André Danican Philidor (1726–1795), the leading chess player in the second half of the eighteenth century in France and England. Stamma lost eight, drew one, and won one. Stamma died in London about eight years later.

Stamma's most important contribution to chess was his books' introduction into Europe of the algebraic chess notation with which he had become familiar in the Middle East—this is explained in figure 6.59.

The above information was mainly sourced from: Eales, Richard. *Chess: The History of a Game*. London: B T Batsford, 1985, and from websites georgianlondon. com, wikipedia.org, and actonbooks.com.

Figure 6.57   Stamma pieces in blackwood (*Acacia melanoxylon*) and Manchurian pear (*Pyrus ussuriensis*). The knight's pot-helm piece symbol is cut aslant.

Figure 6.58 Slaughter's Coffee House, *center*, at 74–75 St. Martin's Lane in London. It was founded by Thomas Slaughter in 1692, and was the leading venue for English chess players during the first seven decades of the 18th century. The building was demolished in 1843 to allow the construction of Cranbourn Street.

After its founder's death, a rival New Slaughters was opened at 82 St. Martin's Lane. The original Slaughter's then became known as Old Slaughter's.

In 1822 and 1824 meetings were held at Old Slaughter's which resulted in the formation of the Society for the Prevention of Cruelty to Animals. In 1840 Queen Victoria gave permission to add the royal *R* so that the society's initials became RSPCA.

Cabinetmaker Thomas Chippendale rented premises opposite in 1753.

Sourced from Wikimedia Commons.

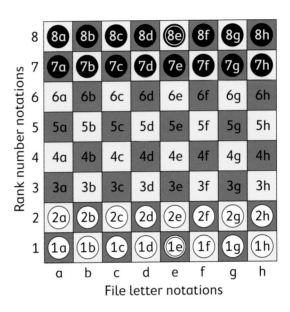

Figure 6.59 The current chessboard standard algebraic notation or SAN required by the FIDE (Fédération Internationale des Échecs or World Chess Federation). It's based upon the notation introduced into Europe by Stamma, and is used to define the positions and movements of chessmen.

Chess was originally conceived as a stylised battle between two Indian armies. This military association continues. Thus the horizontal rows of squares are called *ranks* and are numbered, and the vertical columns of squares are called *files* and are lettered.

The starting positions for the two sides are shown by the black and white circles. The kings' starting positions are denoted by the internal circles. The white side moves first to start a game.

6.6.1 Design

The pencil gauges for the Stamma design are shown in figure 6.60.

Figure 6.60 The pencil gauges for the six Stamma pieces.

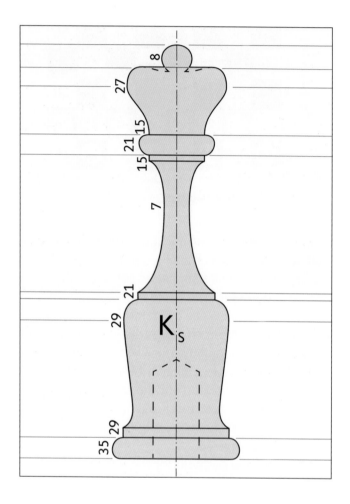

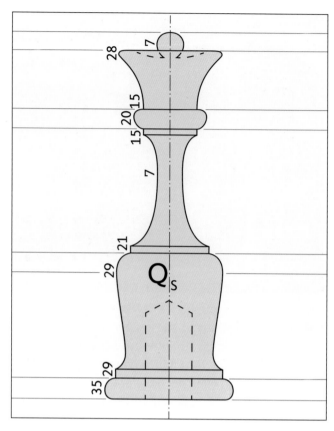

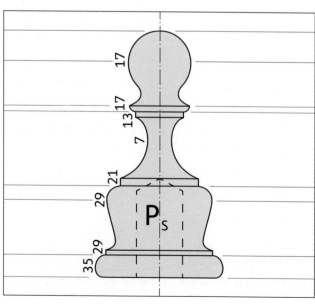

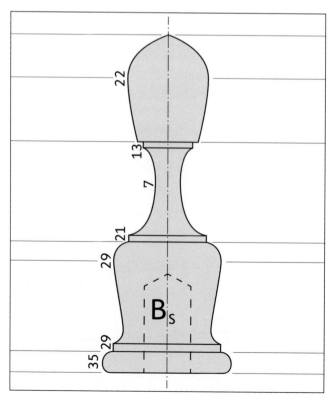

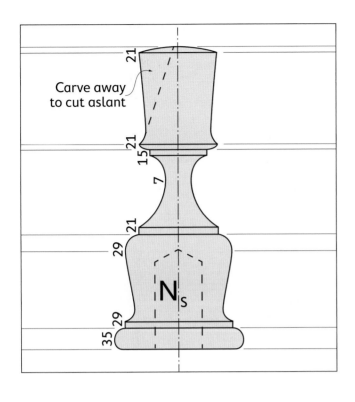

Carve away to cut aslant

21
21
15
7
21
29
29
35

N S

6.6.2 Making

After it's been bored, each man can each be finish-turned while still chucked at its top end. Additional support can be provided by a live center with a conical nose. Other chucking options for finish-turning include turning between centers, and chucking by the leading holes using one of the chucks shown in figures 4.1 to 4.4.

To complete any finish-turning on mens' tops and for polishing the men could be cantilevered from one of the chucks shown in figures 4.1 to 4.4, or pushed onto a wooden pin much as shown in figure 6.46.

6.7 ENDNOTES

1. List, Larry. *The Imagery of Chess Revisited*. New York: George Braziller, 2005.

2. Gombrich, E.H. *The Sense of Order*. Oxford: Phaidon Press, 1979.

3. Keene R.D. and Coles R.N. *Howard Staunton the English World Chess Champion*. St. Leonards on Sea: British Chess Magazine Ltd, 1975.

4. Dean, George. *Chess Masterpieces*. New York: Abrams, 2010, pp 13, 86, 81, 145, 156, 183, 222, 257, and 259.

5. Schwarz, Arturo. *Man Ray: the Rigour of Imagination*. London: Thames and Hudson, 1977.

6. List, Larry. *The Imagery of Chess Revisited*. New York: George Braziller, 2005. p.65. A replica set made in 2004, also with the sides painted black and white, is shown in the same book on pages 64 and 173.

7. Williams, Gareth. *Master Pieces*. London: Quintet Publishing, 2000, p. 131.

8. Most of the above information was sourced from: Eales, Richard. *Chess A History of the Game*. London: B T Batsford, 1985.

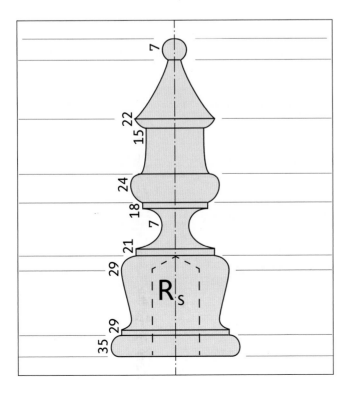

7
22
15
24
18
7
21
29
29
35

R S

6.8   BIBLIOGRAPHY

Pages 163 and 164 of *Turned Chessman* contained a bibliography on chess sets. Listed below are books on chessmen and chess sets published since 2004.

9. Dean, George. *Chess Masterpieces*. New York: Abrams, 2010.

10. Kloprogge, Mathieu and Ine. *Chessmen Art and History*. Amsterdam: Gopher B.V., 2007.

11. List, Larry, editor. *The Imagery of Chess Revisited*. New York: George Braziller, 2005.

12. McLain, Dylan Loeb. *Masterworks: Rare and Beautiful Chess Sets of the World*. London: Fuel Publishing, 2017.

There is a society of chess set collectors called Chess Collectors International which publishes the quarterly journal *The Chess Collector*. The society's website address is http://chesscollectormagazine.sharepoint.com. There are also specialist dealers in chess sets whose websites are worth visiting.

Chapter 7

FRAMES

Turned circular frames were I hope adequately covered on pages 98 to 110 of my book *Woodturning Techniques*. This chapter discusses other types of frame whose construction includes turnings. Although as figure 7.1 shows, such frames were regarded as worthwhile turning subjects in the late 19th century, they seem to have been neglected since. I hope that this chapter will restore interest in them.

The frame types discussed in this chapter are:

1. faux bamboo frames
2. another fully turned frame
3. frames with applied split turnings
4. frames with quadrant corners
5. eared frames
6. frames for a diptych
7. frames with Gothic arches
8. frames constructed from more than one annulus.

But before discussing these frame types, I consider hanging frames, and frame rabbets and sealing.

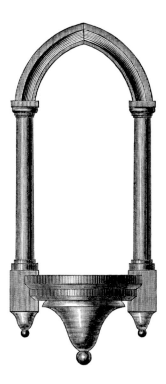

Figure 7.1   Three frame images scanned from: John Jacob Holtzapffel's 1881 book *Hand or Simple Turning.*[1] Before starting to make any of these frames you'll need to do some detailed designing.

7.1 HANGING, RABBETS AND SEALING

This section discusses three topics relevant to most frames: the features provided to hang them, their rabbets, and sealing the back.

Hanging

There are three ways of "hanging" frames:

1. screw through the frame directly into the wall
2. hang the frame from usually one fixing such as a screw or hook either suspended or screwed into a wall as shown in figure 7.1
3. hang with wire (I'll use this term to include cord, line or chain). Proprietory systems are available. Figure 7.2 shows the less expensive wooden picture rail, hook and fishing line method I use at home.

When a frame and its contents are hung using a wire, the frame will attempt to hang with the suspension point, hanging point on the frame, and the center of gravity of the frame and its contents in vertical alignment. Particularly if the hanging point is not near the top of the frame, the frame will therefore want to tilt forwards. This may be desirable if the frame is high on a wall.

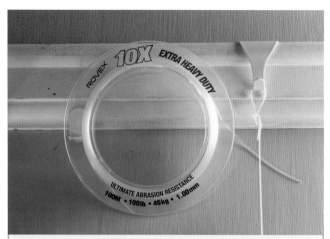

Figure 7.3   An inexpensive hanging system: wooden picture rail, picture hooks, and fishing line. The knot in the fishing line is a figure-of-eight loop.

Figure 7.4   The rear of an upper frame corner showing a small brass ring hanger (one of several types of hanger commercially available), a brad tapped or forced into the side of the top rail's rabbet to hold in the frame contents, and Kikusui self-adhesive paper sealing tape.

Rabbets

A frame will usually need a rabbet large enough, particularly in depth, to accomodate the contents and the associated fixings used to keep the contents securely in place. I usually allow a 10 x 10 mm rabbet, although smaller rabbets are often sufficient.

A frame's primary content can be:

Figure 7.2   The arrangement I use to hang a frame directly from a screw projecting from a wall. The diameter of the steel washer which has been twice drilled and countersunk is 32 mm.

- an image. This may be on card, paper, board or canvas on a stretcher
- a mirror (you should then black the front face of the rabbet)
- some other object such as a document, a plaque, medal, panel of stained glass, tiles, a tapestry, an embroidery or a quilt

Additional associated contents might include a slip, a mat, and/or clear glass:

Sealing

A common way to seal the back of a frame to prevent insects, bacteria etc. getting in is with Kikusui paper tape which is widely available from framing suppliers (figure 7.3).

7.2   A FAUX BAMBOO FRAME

In 2008 I bought the mirror frame shown in figure 7.5 for 6 euros in the Sunday open-air antiques market held in Nantes in north-west France.

In this section I'll give some background to bamboo, and bamboo furniture, and then describe how to make a replica of the mirror.

7.2.1   Bamboo

With over 10,000 species, the *Poaceae* or *Gramineae* (one of the four grass families) is the fifth largest family of flowering plants. Members of its subfamily, the *Bambusoideae*, are native throughout the tropics, and most commonly in Asia. They have woody stems, and

THE BAMBOO.

Figure 7.6   A thicket of *Dendrocalamus giganteous*.[2]

Figure 7.5   Front view of the antique faux bamboo mirror. Turned from European beech (*Fagus sylvatica*), the wood was walnut stained and French polished. The size of the frame to its tips is 348 mm wide x 408 mm high.

the largest species, *Dendrocalamus giganteous* can reach a height of 30 meters (figure 7.6). Some species of bamboo can grow 90 centimeters in 24 hours.

The young shoots of bamboo are edible (figure 7.7). The stems had and have many uses including blowpipes, paper making, musical instruments, containers, scaffolding and furniture.

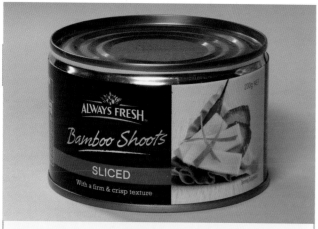

Figure 7.7   A tin of bamboo shoots.

7.2.2   Introduction of bamboo to the West

Sino-European trade was fostered from the 9th century by merchants, mostly Arab and Persian, who settled in Canton (now called Guangzhou). The founding of the Mongol dynasty by Jenghis Khan in 1215, and its subsequent consolidation by Kublai Khan made trade in luxury goods including silk between China and Europe a little easier along the land routes called collectively the Silk Road.

Europe's fascination with the Orient was stimulated by Marco Polo's account *Il Milione*, known in English as *Travels of Marco Polo*, published after Polo returned to Venice in 1295 from his 24-year sojourn. Further impetus was given by the publication of *The Travels of Sir John Mandeville* between 1457 and 1371—the book is now known to be largely a product of the author Jan de Langhe's fertile imagination.

Until the mid-16th century the entrepot for Europe's trade with China was Venice. However in 1514 the

Portuguese sailed into Canton. Trade between Portugal and China grew despite the indifference of the latter. In 1557 Portuguese merchants were expelled from Canton, but granted permission to settle on the tiny peninsula of Macau, also spelt Macao (figure 7.8).

The Dutch East India Company, the world's first joint-stock company chartered in 1602, and The Company of Merchants of London trading into the East Indies (the English East India Company) chartered on 31 December 1600, were both founded to break the Portuguese monopoly on oriental sea trade. The French East India Company was in turn founded in 1660 to break the English and Dutch trading strangleholds.

The English East India Company's Captain Weddell reached Canton in 1636, but wasn't permitted to trade there. Not until 1715 was the Company allowed to

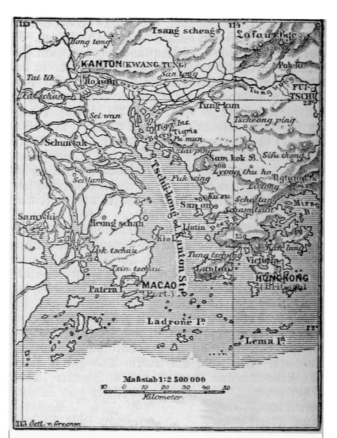

Figure 7.8   The estuary of the Pearl River on the southern coast of China showing Macau, Hong Kong and Canton.
Sourced from Wikimedia Commons.

Figure 7.9 The European and American hongs at Canton in about 1820. A hong is one or more buildings in China which form a warehouse, depot or manufactory.
Sourced from Wikimedia Commons.

and Darly; and Sir William Chambers' *Chinese Designs of Buildings, Furniture, Dresses, Machines and Utensils* (1757).

The popularity of exotic styles in the decorative arts and architecture of Europe waxed and waned through the 18th and 19th centuries, but was particularly strong between 1870 and WWI. This was catalysed by the opportunity to trade with Japan, prised open by US Navy Commodore Matthew Calbraith Perry in 1853 and 1854. Within ten years Japan was exporting some bamboo furniture, and also bamboo stems for conversion into furniture. So popular did bamboo furniture become that in England between 1869 and 1935 up to 150 English businesses were making it from stems imported from Japan.[3]

The interest in Chinoiserie and Japanese-inspired design and artefacts (the two tended to be both con-

found its first factory or hong in Canton (figure 7.9). From 1757 until Britain forced the handover of Hong Kong in 1842 after the First Opium War, Canton was the only port in China at which European and American merchants were permitted to trade

7.2.3 European interest in oriental furniture

Although the earliest extant bamboo furniture dates from the Sung dynasty (960—1279 AD), its production started much earlier and continues in Asia today (figure 7.10). Once sea trade between Asia and Europe was established in the 17th and 18th centuries, bamboo furniture and artefacts, and bamboo stems, were increasingly exported to Europe and North America. The use of oriental motifs, ornamental forms and materials in European furniture, decorative arts and architecture became popular. Not only were oriental goods imported, but European craftsmen exploited the Chinese and other Asian styles in their own furniture, ceramics, plasterwork, etc. This was aided by such publications as *Treatise of Japanning and Varnishing* (1688) by John Stalker and George Parker; Thomas Chippendale's *Gentleman and Cabinet-Maker's Director* published in 1754 (figure 7.11); *New Book of Chinese Designs* (1754) by Edwards

Figure 7.10 A Japanese bamboo armoire in the collection of the Musee du Quai Branly in Paris.
Sourced from Wikimedia Commons.

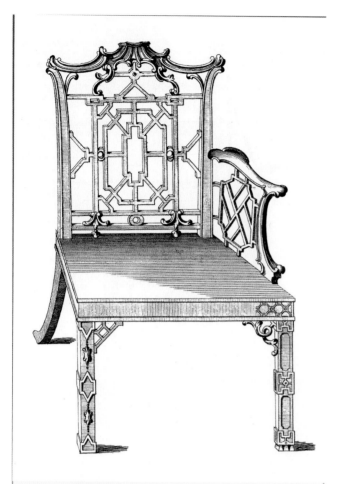

Figure 7.11   A Chinese chair design from plate XXVII of Thomas Chippendale's *The Gentleman & Cabinet-Maker's Director.*
    Scanned from the Dover facsimile edition.[4]

Figure 7.12   Rear view of the antique faux bamboo mirror showing the rabbeted rails and sides.

fused and fused) was important throughout Europe and in North America. In France, faux bamboo turning in beech, both for structural members and applied mouldings, was especially popular as my mirror frame purchase confirms.

7.2.4   The frame's design

Figures 7.12 and 7.13 show more detail of the antique frame, and figure 7.14 shows the design of a quarter of the frame. All the frame's spindles have the same 27-mm-maximum outside diameter. The two major internodal lengths are shorter in the horizontal spindles (72 mm) than in the vertical spindles (102 mm). Ideally

Figure 7.13   Rear view of a mirror joint showing how the horizontal spindle passes through the vertical spindle, and each horizontal finial is glued onto a pin turned on an end of a horizontal spindle.

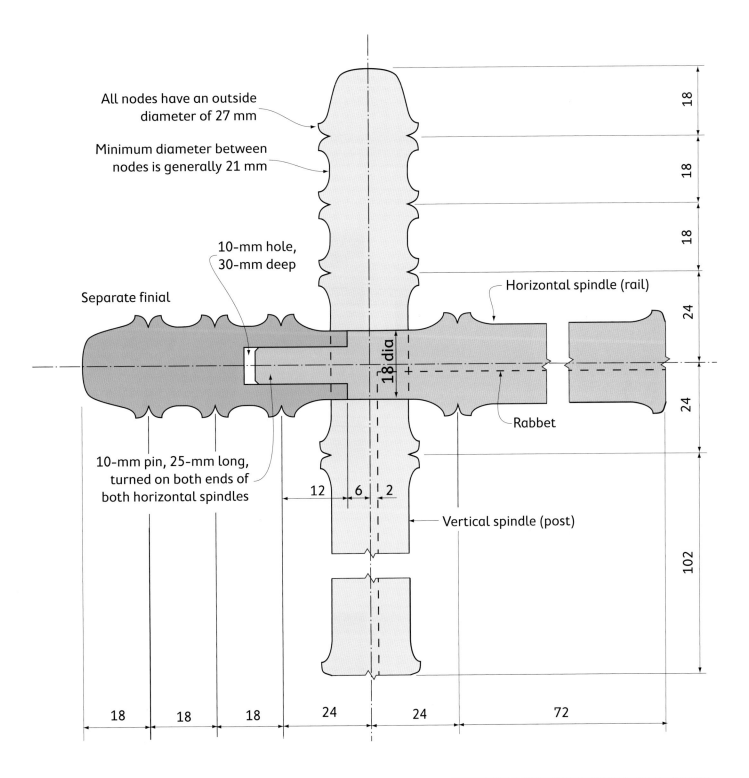

All nodes have an outside diameter of 27 mm

Minimum diameter between nodes is generally 21 mm

10-mm hole, 30-mm deep

Separate finial

10-mm pin, 25-mm long, turned on both ends of both horizontal spindles

Horizontal spindle (rail)

18 dia

Rabbet

Vertical spindle (post)

18

18

18

24

24

102

12 6 2

18 18 18 24 24 72

Figure 7.14 A section through a quarter of the faux bamboo mirror frame showing the construction and dimensions.

when designing faux bamboo mirrors of other sizes, the lengths between nodes should be approximately equal in both the horizontal and vertical spindles, and the spindle lengths made different by varying the number of nodes.

Note the design detailing at the nodes: it's quite subtle and closely follows that of real bamboo (figure 7.15).

The vertical spindles have a node where each horizontal spindle runs through to effectively increase the strength in that region.

Figure 7.15   A node in black bamboo.

7.2.5   Making the frame

My antique frame was turned from European beech (*Fagus sylvatica*). I turned my copy from Australian mountain ash, *Eucalyptus regnans*. If you're going to clear finish or stain your frame this should influence your choice of wood. If you're going to paint your frame, almost any wood will do.

The workpieces need a dressed cross section of 28 x 28 mm minimum for the two vertical and two horizontal spindles, and for the four finials. (The finials are intended to resemble the knobbly club-shaped roots of bamboo.) The workpieces for the vertical posts and the top and bottom horizontal members called *rails* should be about 60-mm-longer than their members' net finished lengths. This allows square cross section waste ends to be left to locate the spindles when the rabbets for the mirror glass are routed. Each finial workpiece should be about 30-mm-longer than the net length of a finial to allow about a 20-mm length to be held in a scroll chuck for boring.

When dressing the workpieces, mark the face and face edge surfaces, especially at the ends of the four spindle workpieces because those markings will be needed to ensure that the spindles are in the correct axial orientation when the rabbets are being routed. You can of course vary the dimensions and the number of nodes of a frame.

Making the frame is explained in figures 7.16 to 7.28.

Figure 7.16   About to drill the 18-mm-diameter holes through a post workpiece. I use the ex-screwdriver ground to a point (*shown left*) to press conical holes to locate drill points and drive and tail centers.

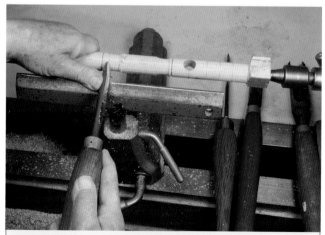

Figure 7.17   Hand steadying a post when cutting an apophyge profile (see figure 7.48) at a node with a detail gouge.

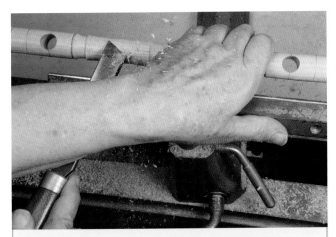

Figure 7.18 Hand steadying when planing between nodes. My left wrist is locating and steadying the skew on the toolrest while my left hand is steadying the slender spindle.

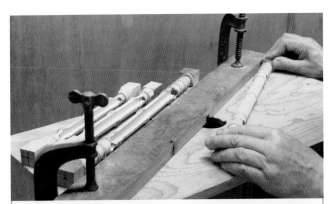

Figure 7.21 Routing the rabbets into the posts and rails. The rails are then cut to length, and the posts are rechucked between centers so that their ends can be finish-turned. After the posts have been parted off, some hand finishing of the ends will be needed.

Figure 7.19 A post finish-turned apart from ends which are left square, and will be completed and polished after routing.

Figure 7.22 Chucking a finial workpiece.

Figure 7.20 A rail after the first turning operation. The pins haven't been turned down to their finished diameter of 10 mm so that the rail is stiff enought to have its rabbet routed.

Figure 7.23 Scraping a conical recess into the already flattened end of a finial workpiece with a skew's long point so that the drill will bore truly axially.

Figure 7.25 After all the finials have been partly finish-turned, the workpieces are transposed and reverse chucked on a wooden pin turned in waste wood. The finish-turning of the finial workpieces is then completed as shown in figure 7.26 .

Figure 7.24 A finial bored to the depth of the green tape being partly finish-turned.

Figure 7.26 Finish-turning the pins on the ends of the two horizontal spindles.

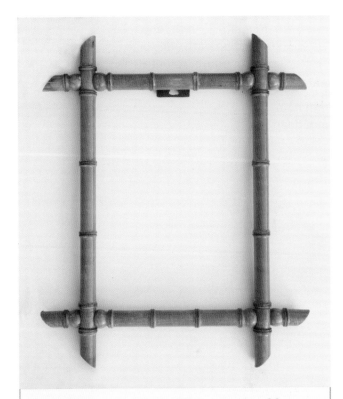

7.3   A LARGER FAUX BAMBOO FRAME

Figures 7.29 to 7.32 show an antique, faux-bamboo mirror with different corner detailing. However its construction is essentially the same as that shown earlier in figure 7.14.

Figure 7.27   About to fix the mirror into the frame showing the mirror glass (with the green coating on its rear surface), the protective cardboard backing, the pins which will be hammered into the sides of the rabbets to secure the mirror and backing, and the loop of hanging wire which passes through two small drilled holes. For mirrors the surface of the rabbet should be blackened to prevent the bare wood being visible when the mirror is viewed from the front.

Figure 7.29   A slightly-different style of faux bamboo mirror. Its overall size is 570-mm-wide x 690-mm-high.

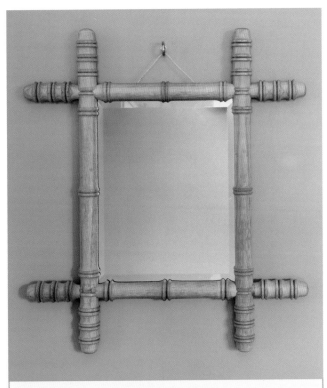

Figure 7.28   The finished mirror.

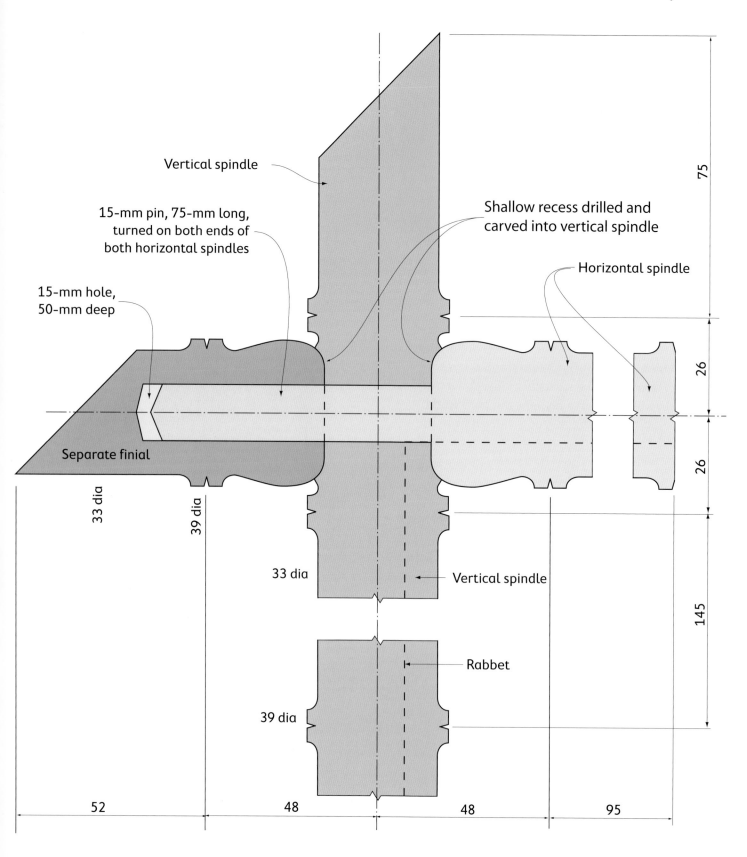

Vertical spindle

15-mm pin, 75-mm long,
turned on both ends of
both horizontal spindles

Shallow recess drilled and
carved into vertical spindle

Horizontal spindle

15-mm hole,
50-mm deep

Separate finial

33 dia

39 dia

33 dia

Vertical spindle

39 dia

Rabbet

75

26

26

145

52

48

48

95

Figure 7.30   Details of a frame corner drawn full size.

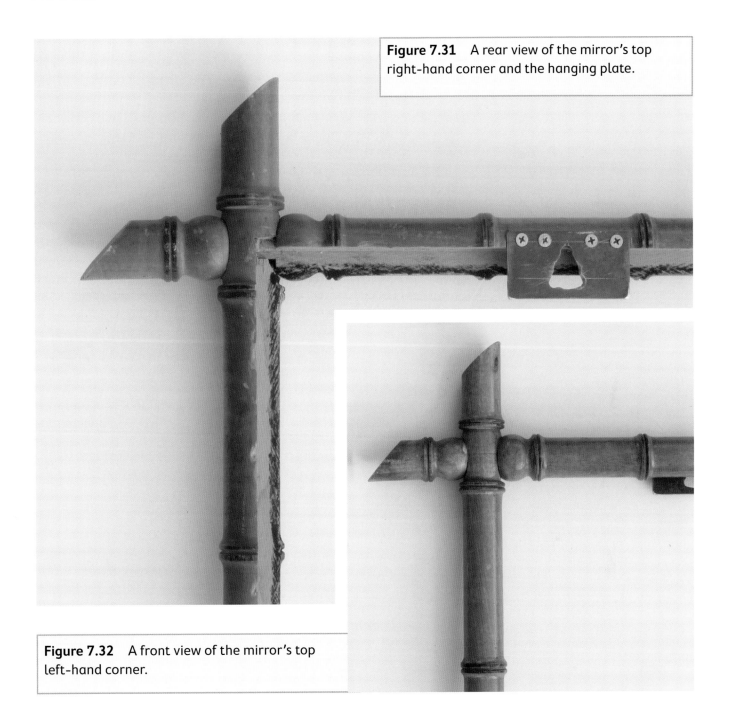

Figure 7.31 A rear view of the mirror's top right-hand corner and the hanging plate.

Figure 7.32 A front view of the mirror's top left-hand corner.

7.4 ANOTHER FULLY-TURNED FRAME

In this section I'll describe how to make a rectangular frame with turned cylindrical posts and rails, and with turned corner blocks which have transverse grain. Figure 7.33 shows the clear-polished version I made it to house an 1881 engraving of a turner operating a treadle lathe. Figure 7.34 shows the painted version I made to house an oil painting.

Figure 7.33 The corners disks are in an unknown wood, and the spindles are in New Guinea rosewood, *Pterocarpus indicus*.

The engraving of the woodturner operating a treadle lathe is scanned from *The Book of English Trades and Library of the Useful Arts*, London: G. and W. B. Whittaker, 1824, p. 406.

7.4.1 Design

Figure 7.35 shows the frame's design. Because I wanted to provide 10 mm x 10 mm rabbets in the frame spindles, and I had a 1-inch-diameter drill, I also made the spindles' finished diameter 1 inch.

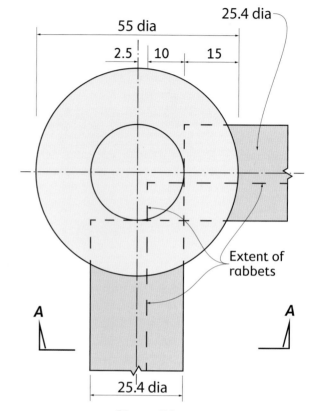

Plan of frame corner

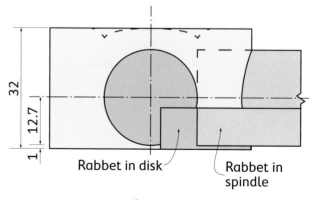

Section A–A

Figure 7.35 Details of a frame corner. The finished length of a side spindle is the full length of the frame rabbet required less twice the width of the rabbet.

Figure 7.34 A frame turned in radiata pine (*Pinus radiata*) and painted.

7.4.2 Making

This frame has only two types of wooden components, the corner disks and the posts and rails. Making the corner disks will be described first.

Making the corner disks

The corner disks can be made using one of two methods:

1. Prepare square blocks slightly oversize, drill the two holes in each to house the spindle ends (figure 7.36), drill the hole to chuck the disk on a screwchuck, bandsaw the corner waste away, and then finish-turn the disks. The problem with this method is that you're likely to get tear-out at the hole entrances. I rather like the onomatopoetic term *spelch* which English turner Reg Sherwin used for this sort of tear-out.

2. Finish-turn the corner disks on a screwchuck. Before dechucking each disk, mark the two lines along which the hole centers lie, ideally using your lathe's indexing facility (figure 7.37). When marking these lines ensure that the grain direction of each disk in the completed frame will align. Then drill the holes, ideally using a jig and a drilling machine (figures. 7.38, 7.39 and 7.40).

3. Use a marking gauge to mark the thickness which will have to be chiselled away from the inside part of each corner disk (figure 7.41).

Figure 7.37 Marking the horizontal lines along which the centers of the two holes lie.

Figure 7.36 Drilling a corner disk.

Figure 7.38 The jig for drilling the corner disks. The vertical pencil line on the back plate springs from the bottom of the vee.

Figure 7.39 The jig clamped in place on the drilling machine's table.

Figure 7.41 Marking the height of the waste which will be chiselled away to form the corner recess after the frame has been glued together.

Figure 7.40 A disk clamped for drilling. The line along the disk meets the vertical line drawn on the jig's black plate.

Making the posts and rails

The spindles are straightforward. Dress two faces of each spindle workpiece at 90° to each other. Each workpiece should be about 50-mm-longer than its spindle's finished length. Mark the turning centers off the two dressed faces with a marking gauge. With the point of a bradawl or similar make a small conical hole where the two lines cross so that you can center the spindles accurately. Turn a test diameter in a piece of scrap wood so that you can caliper the spindles to the diameter which will fit snuggly into the holes in the corner disks. Turn the lengths to the hole diameter leaving the last 15 mm at each end unturned. Mark the accurate finished length of each spindle with a pencil or a skews long point (figure 7.42). Then make two cuts on a saw bench to cut the rabbet in each spindle (figure 7.43). Rechuck each spindle in your lathe, and nearly part-through at the finished length. Then cut the waste pommels off each spindle.

Polishing and assembly

You can polish, paint or even guild the frame after it has been glued together. However it's better to polish each component after it has been finish-turned. Any between-coats sanding can then be done in the lathe. In this case don't polish the areas on the ends of the spindles which will be glued into the corner disks.

Check that all goes together nicely, then glue the frame together on a flat surface checking that the frame is truly rectangular, not rhomboid.

When the glue has hardened, chisel away the corner recess waste from the corner disks (figure 7.44). Fix the hangers and install the contents (figure 7.45).

Figure 7.43 Showing a spindle after cutting the sides of the rabbet on a table saw. The right-hand and bottom faces of the workpiece shown here were the reference faces. Alternatively the rabbet could be cut on a router table.

Figure 7.42 A spindle turned and polished. Note the face marks marked on the two faces of the end pommels and that the ends of the finished length aren't polished.

Figure 7.44 The back of a corner showing the rabbets in the spindles and the recess chiselled into the corner disk.

Figure 7.45 A frame corner showing a hanger screwed to the back of a corner disk. To fix the content into the frame I tap in tacks. I use the hammer shown which has a flat ground onto side of the striking part of the head.

7.5 SPLIT-SPINDLE FRAMES

This section will start by showing two earlier examples of ornamental applied split turnings, before briefly discussing the geometry of engaged columns. It then shows five antique split-turned frames before describing how two particular frame designs are made.

7.5.1 Split turnings

Spindles split along their lengths, usually called *split turnings*, have been applied to ornament flat surfaces for more than two-and-a-half thousand years. In the earliest example I've found, shown in figure 7.46, a split turning is applied to the rear upright of the throne of Xerxes. More recently, case furniture was ornamented with applied split turnings figure 7.47.

In classical architecture it has long been recognised that an engaged column (one which is joined to a wall) appears somewhat feeble if its projection measured at the height of the bottom of the column shaft (just above the apophyge in most column orders as figure 7.48 shows) is exactly half the column shaft diameter at that height Therefore as figure 7.49 shows, a larger proportion than 50% is typically used although different authorities recommend different projections. Sebastiano Serlio (1475–

Figure 7.46 A limestone relief showing a split turning on the back post or stile of a throne carved in the first half of the 6th century BC. This limestone carving lines the northern staircase to the apadana (many-columned hypostyle hall) at Persepolis in Iran.

Sourced from Wikimedia Commons.

Figure 7.47 An oak sideboard with applied split turnings made in England circa. 1690.

Scanned from: Litchfield, Frederick. *Illustrated History of Furniture*. London: Truslove & Hanson, 1893, p. 97.

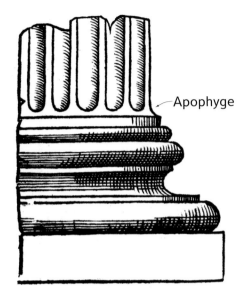

Figure 7.48 The lower part of a fluted classical column. The transition curve between the straight part of the column shaft and the fillet immediately above the top of the column base is an apophyge.

Scanned from: Serlio, Sebastiano. *The Five Books of Architecture*. New York: Dover Publications, 1982, third Booke folio 52. (Originally published in 1611.)

Figure 7.49 Engaged columns with projecting cross sections greater than semicircles on the church of Saint Guiliano in Venice.

Scanned from: Sturgis, Russell et al. *Sturgis' Illustrated Dictionary of Architecture and Building*. Mineola: Dover Publications, 1989, volume 1 of 3, plate XXXII.

1554) for example recommended 68% while Andrea Palladio (1541–1580) recommended 60%.[5, 6] However, because split turnings in wood are typically produced by splitting (unlike masonary engaged columns), departing from the usual 50/50 split would double the number of turnings needed and is therefore uncommon.

7.5.2 The technique of split turning

The techniques for producing split turnings were described on pages 13 to 17 of my 2001 book *Woodturning Techniques*; those pertinent to frames are also described below. (Two later books with the same title by other authors have been published.)

Splitting a turning longitudinally by sawing can be difficult to accomplish accurately, can be dangerous, and results in a loss of wood in the saw kerf and through any subsequent necessary planing of the sawn surfaces. The preferred alternative is to use a paper joint.

Figure 7.50 illustrates how to produce split turnings which are semicircular in cross section. But the cross sections of split turning don't have to be uniformly semicircular. If using a single paper joint, it need not run along a diameter of the turning nor be parallel to the axis of the turning. You can also produce split turnings by using more than one paper joint, and those paper joints need not be parallel. However if a split turning's cross section is less than half that of the whole turning, what I'll call the *edge angle* (shown in figure 7.50) will be less than 90°. Therefore when riving down the paper joint (shown in figure 7.51), the wood along the edge is more likely to break away.

Good quality brown paper is preferred for paper joints. It is thick enough and not so porous that the glue (usually PVA, and shown green in figure 7.50) which is smeered onto the faces of the two wooden component parts which it separates won't penetrate through the full thickness of the paper when the combined workpiece is clamped. The clamping should not be too fierce or the glue may be squeezed out of the joint or forced through the full thickness of the paper.

The brown paper joint is not the only technique which can be used to produce split turnings. If the wood components remain sufficiently stiff, mechanical fixings can be employed either with or without paper joints to hold the components together during the turning.

When turning a split-turning workpiece:

- Don't turn too vigorously and don't have the lathe speed excessively high.

Figure 7.51 Tapping a thin-bladed knife down a paper joint to separate the spindle into two split turnings.

- Use a cup/ring live tail center in preference to one with a conical tip.
- If using a spur drive center, ensure that the spurs are located so as to not rive the paper joint.

In the next three chapter sections I'll discuss two frame types: those where the split turnings are mitered at the corners, and those in which the split turnings span between upstanding corner blocks.

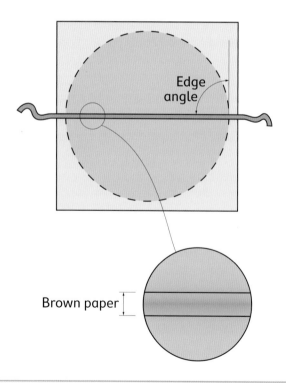

Figure 7.50 Producing two split turnings of semicircular cross section with a paper joint. The ideal extent of glue penetration is shown in green.

7.5.3 A split-turned frame with mitered corners

Figure 7.52 shows a frame in which the applied split turnings are mitered at the corners. I'll first discuss the design, then the making.

Figure 7.52 A rectangular frame with applied split turnings.

Design

The underframe's posts and rails have the same rectangular cross section (ignoring the rabbet). The corners can be mitered or butt-jointed, or have corner blocks of the same thickness into which the rails and posts are dowelled.

The split turnings shown in figure 7.52 are rows of identical beads, but I decided not to carry the beads into the corners. To ensure that all fits together as intended, you'll need to determine all dimensions, including the width of the beads, exactly. Note, the length of the mitered surfaces in a 90° corner is 1.414 times the width of either of the members.

Making

Apart from the need to work accurately, this type of frame presents no particular problems. If the frame is to be clear polished, take care not to get glue onto exposed surfaces. It's best to polish the turnings in the lathe before splitting them. I also polish the posts and rails before fixing the split turnings using glue and/or screws. If using glue, I leave a band unpolished along the centers of the post and rail surfaces.

The split turnings are usually glued, or screwed, or screwed-and-glued to the posts and rails. If gluing only, I apply glue sparingly in a narrow strip along the center of the split turnings' flat faces and along the centers of the posts and rails. I then, as shown in figure 7.53, use masking tape to hold the split turnings in position until the glue has set.

If screwing or screwing-and-gluing, I find that if I screw through the drilled and countersunk holes without first taping the the split turnings in their intended positions, those turnings often shift from their intended positions.

Note, when gluing end grain or mitered surfaces, prime the surfaces with glue, and allow it set before applying glue again and clamping the joint(s) together.

Figure 7.53 The frame shown in figure 7.52 with the split turnings glued and taped onto the frame members.

7.5.4 Antique split-turned frames with corner blocks

Frames with split turnings were especially fashionable in the eastern states of the United States in the 18th and 19th centuries. This was confirmed when I chanced upon the Northeast Auctions catalogue for the August 2008 sale in Manchester, New Hampshire, of the late Michael Schnall's collection of early Americana. Figures 7.54 to 7.58 show split-spindle mirror frames from that catalogue.

All the frames shown in figures 7.54 to 7.58 have corner blocks. Using corner blocks avoids the problem that the mitered corners of rectangular frames, particularly if the frame posts and rails are wide, are likely to open with changes in the wood's moisture content. The next subsection describes making such a frame.

Figure 7.55 A stencil-decorated looking glass with applied split turnings, made circa. 1830, height 495 mm, width 394 mm.

Figure 7.54 A Pennsylvania-made, polychrome, split-spindle looking glass, circa. 1840, height 445 mm, width 387 mm.

Figure 7.56 A paint-decorated, split-spindle looking glass with an eglomise tablet of a house and trees. The term *eglomise* recalls the 18th-century French decorator Jean-Baptiste Glomy, and means 'made of glass and painted on its rear face'. The frame is 610-mm high and 305-mm wide. Stamped brass rosettes are applied to the corner blocks.

Figure 7.57 A mahogany, split-spindle, looking glass possibly made in Newburyport circa. 1830. The frame is 610-mm high and 305-mm wide.

7.5.5 A contemporary split-turned frame with corner blocks

Figures 7.54, 7.55 and 7.56 show frames with split turnings whose polychrome decoration was produced by painting. The frame with corner blocks in figure 7.59 achieves its polychrome effect by employing woods of different colors. To retain the color contracts I polished the frame with water-based polurethane. This polish is clear, not tinted like the more common oil-based polurethane. Note that end grain absorbs polish more readily and will usually become darker than polished side grain. The patera inlaid into the corner blocks are therefore transverse grained (turned from disks cut from planks).

Figure 7.58 A New England, gilt, split-spindle looking glass with an eglomise tablet of a woman. The frame is 1295-mm high and 711-mm wide.

The cross sections of the turned posts and rails appear to be larger than semicircles.

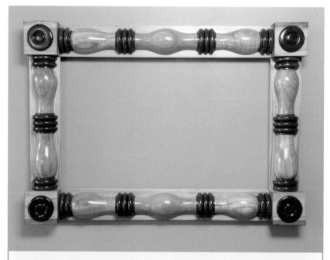

Figure 7.59 A mirror frame with corner blocks and applied split turnings. Its posts and rails are radiata pine (*Pinus radiata*); the dark wood is black apple (*Planchonella autralis*), and the paler split turnings are silky oak (*Grevillea robusta*). The frame's overall size is 430 mm x 612 mm.

Design

The design of the figure 7.59 frame is shown in figure 7.60. The corner blocks should be a little thicker than the thickness of the posts or rails plus the thickness of the split turnings where they abut the corner blocks.

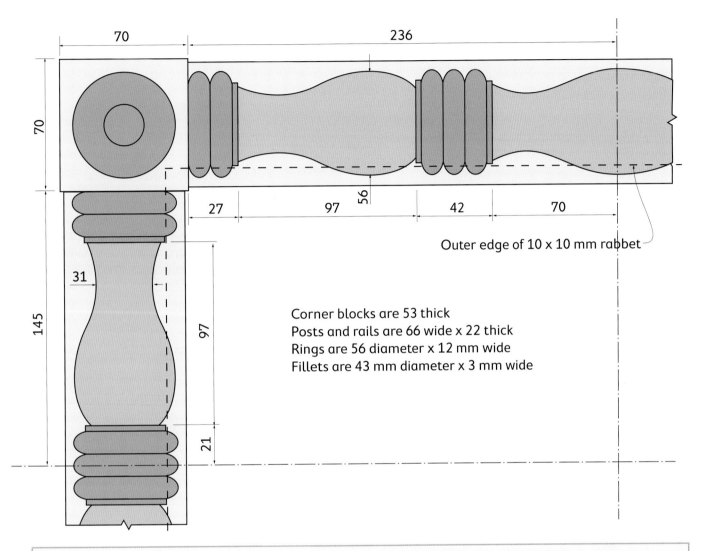

Figure 7.60 The dimensions of the frame shown in figure 7.59. The frame can be hung in portrait or landscape orientation.

Making

The steps for making a frame such as that in figures 7.59 and 7.60 are:

- Prepare the posts, rails and corner blocks. Cut the rabbets along the inside bottom edges of the posts and rails. Drill the ends of the posts and rails and the corner blocks for the dowels.
- Chisel out the inside corners of the corner blocks so that the rabbet is continuous.
- Drill the the corner blocks for chucking on a screw-chuck. Chuck the corner blocks one by one to turn the 5-mm-deep recess to house its patera.

- Turn the patera on a screwchuck, checking that each fits nicely into its recess. Glue each patera into its recess.
- Dry assemble the frame to check its accuracy.
- Prepare the workpieces for split turning. I glued longish lengths together using paper joints and then cut the individual workpieces to length.
- Finish-turn each split-turning workpiece checking its length. Polish and then split them. Note, you could produce the split spindles with spigots and mating holes to make positioning easier.

- Rub, chisel and sand off any paper left on the split turnings, or, if a water-soluble glue was used, soak it first.
- Mark center lines along the top surfaces of the posts and rails with a marking gauge.
- Locate the split spindles in their final positions, then very lightly draw around them on the surfaces of the posts and rails in pencil. Remove the split turnings and draw more heavily about 5 mm inside the previous lines.
- If you'll be screwing the split turnings onto the frame, drill and countersink the appropriate screw holes,
- Black the inside of the rabbet if the frame is to house a mirror.
- Polish the corner blocks and their glued-in patera, and the surfaces of the posts and rails outside the heavier pencil outlines of the split turnings.
- Glue the posts, rails, and corner blocks together. Apply and fix the split turnings as explained on page 95.
- Install the hanging facilities.
- Fix in the frame's contents.

7.6   QUADRANT-CORNER FRAMES

Rectangular frames don't have to have "square" corners. as figure 7.61 shows. If the cross sections of the posts and rails are identical, an annulus with the same cross section can be turned and quartered.

If the sides and rails have a moulded profile there are two ways to match that: with an internal or an external gauge. An internal gouge is more accurate, but needs an open radial joint or saw cut. However if you use several screws to hold the workpiece hard against the backing plate, and don't run the lathe too fast, there's little risk of the workpiece coming off. The process is fully explained on pages 104 to 106.

The posts, rails and corner quadrants of the frame in figure 7.61 are constructed in three layers of radiata pine, each 16-mm-thick. The components of each post and rail are screwed togther. Each corner quadrant is constructed from a quarter of three disks. The corner quadrants are joined to the posts and rails with dowels.

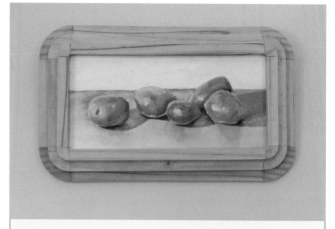

Figure 7.61   A frame with quadrant corners. Its overall size is 490 x 290 mm.

7.7   EARED FRAMES

To avoid any copyright litigation I haven't named the type of frame corner shown in figure 7.62 after a Californian cartoon rodent. Instead I'm calling the resulting frames *eared*. Whether the eared frame is an aesthetically-pleasing invention I leave you to judge. Relatively narrower frame sides and rails would result in less dominating ears. The concept could be thought to imply, as does the quadrant-corner frame above, that, if the surface coloring is uniform, the frame is formed from a continuous ribbon of material.

Figure 7.62   An eared frame constructed from Sydney blue gum (*Eucalyptus saligna*) and radiata-pine plywood.

Design

Figure 7.63 shows the design of the frame in figure 7.62.

One of the realities of designing is after you believe that you've invented something, as figure 7.64 demonstrates, an earlier example turns up.

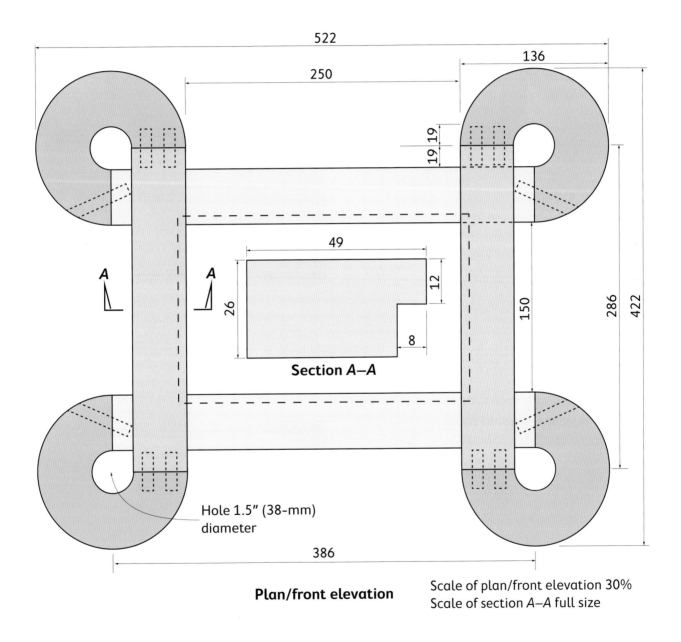

Section A–A

Hole 1.5″ (38-mm) diameter

Plan/front elevation

Scale of plan/front elevation 30%
Scale of section A–A full size

Figure 7.63 The design of the eared frame pictured in figure 7.62.

The holes for the pairs of dowels were obviously drilled before gluing on the ears. Then, as each ear was glued on, the hole for its diagonal dowel was drilled, and the dowel glued in. After the glue had set the projecting ends of the diagonal dowels were trimmed flush.

Figure 7.64   A simplified drawing of a three-eared corner detail from one of the carpet pages in the *Book of Durrow*. This illuminated book was probably created between 650 and 700 AD in Durrow Abbey, and is now in the Library of Trinity College, in Dublin.
     The village of Durrow is in central Ireland.

Figure 7.65   Finish-turning the perimeter of an ear annulus. The active edge (that part of the edge actually cutting) is being traversed at a high side rake.

Making

The frame posts and rails need to be be essentially rectangular because they cross at the corners, although the sides need not be flat nor at right-angles to the top and bottom surfaces. The posts and rails cross by means of halving joints.

Because I intended to paint the frame, I made the ear workpieces by gluing together two thicknesses of 13-mm-thick plywood. I then marked the perimeter of each annulus with compasses, drilled the central 1.5-inch (38-mm)-diameter hole, and bandsawed it out. As shown in figures 7.65 and 7.66, I chucked the workpiece using its hole, and then finish-turned the periphery.

Figure 7.67 shows how I marked out where to cut an ear annulus after the posts and rails had been glued together.

How I fixed each ear piece is explained in the caption to figure 7.63.

Figure 7.66   De-chucking an ear annulus showing how I chucked it on the outside gripping surfaces of the jaws of an engineer's scroll chuck.

Figure 7.67 Scribing where to saw away the waste segment from an ear annulus.

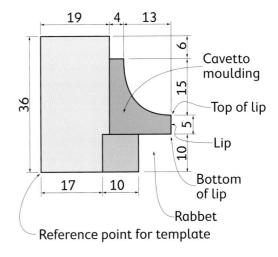

Figure 7.69 Because it's hinged, the diptych frame shown in figure 7.68 can be free-standing.

7.8 DIPTYCH FRAMES

A diptych is a pair of paintings, usually of a husband and wife, hinged together. The two paintings are therefore usually framed. This section describes the design and making of the pair of frames with semicircular tops shown in figures 7.68 and 7.69.

Design

One construction for the straight parts of the frames is shown in figure 7.70. The dimensions for one of the frames is shown in figure 7.71.

Figure 7.68 A frame with semicircular tops for a diptych, here hanging.

Section A–A in figure 7.71

Figure 7.70 A cross section through one of the straight parts of the figure 7.68 frames.

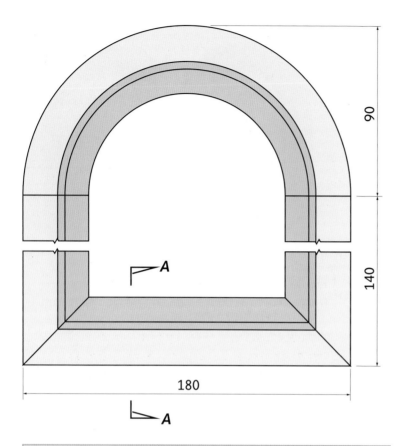

Figure 7.71   A dimensioned, half full-size front elevation of one of the arched frames shown in figures 7.68 and 7.69.

nal template. The internal template is easier to use and more accurate, but requires a radial slit in the workpiece. This slit could be a saw kerf through a one-piece workpiece. Instead, as shown in figure 7.73, I first glued two pieces of wood together; then glued the resulting two pieces together using two thicknesses of veneer to create the slit.

To turn the pair of arches, I first finish-turned the rear of the frame and the rabbet as shown in figure 7.74.

An internal template needs a reference point. It also needs an outer larger outline of the moulding to warn the turner that the turned radial section is approaching the final intended shape.

Making

It doesn't matter whether you match the cross section of the posts and the bottom rail to the arch's cross section or vice versa. The latter is more common. I built up the posts and bottom rail as shown in section *A–A* of figure 7.70. After the glue had set I cut the square ends and miters, and glued them together using miter clamps as shown in figure 7.72.

When turning a circular moulding from a workpiece with transverse grain (a disk cut from a plank) tearout is likely to occur in the two areas where turning is against the grain. To avoid that I glued up the workpiece for the two arches from four pieces of wood as shown in figure 7.73. By having the grain directions as shown, turning against the grain was avoided.

To accurately finish-turn annular mouldings to a specified cross section one can monitor the radial section through the workpiece with an internal or an exter-

Figure 7.72   Gluing together a bottom rail and right-hand post using a Bessey-brand WS3 corner clamp.

Figure 7.73 The second gluing of the arches workpiece. The arrows show the grain directions in the four component pieces.

The two top squares and the two bottom squares were glued together earlier.

Figure 7.75 About to reverse-chuck the workpiece by screwing it onto the specially prepared backing disk. Each of the four screws will be driven into the center of each workpiece segment. The larger diameter recess in the workpiece should neatly locate on the projection turned in the backing disk. The outside diameter of the backing disk has been finish-turned to the intended 180-mm finished outside diameter of the arches.

Figure 7.74 Turning the back (bottom) of the arches workpiece with a 12-mm-diameter detail gouge. The workpiece is mounted on a screwchuck. The turning here is against the grain, but when the workpiece is reverse-chucked turning will be against the grain.

When turning the lip, take the cut well past its top.

Figure 7.76 The template for the arches. The inner line represents the intended profile. The outer line is a warning profile which will alert me that I'm nearly at the final shape and should proceed carefully.

Figure 7.77   Turning the arches is almost completed. A little more needs to be cut away from the cavetto.

7.9   FRAMES WITH GOTHIC ARCHES

The Gothic period in Europe lasted approximately from 1150 to 1450, and was followed by a neo-Gothic period from about 1740 to late in the 19th century. Conveniently for woodturners the Gothic arch was usually composed of two arcs.

Figure 7.78 and 7.80 show a frame of my design in the Gothic style. Its three finials are based upon one shown in: Meyer, Franz Sales. *Handbook of Ornament.* New York: Dover Publications, 1957, p. 180, illustration 5. (Originally published in 1888.)

You can find images of arches and related features which can be incorporated into frames in sources on Gothic architecture (figure 7.79). As figures 7.81 and 7.82 illustrate, art galleries with collections of Gothic art are another rich source.

Figure 7.78   A Gothic-style frame. The overall size is 242 x 408 mm.

Figure 7.79   A sedilia, a group of stone seats for clergy in the south, sun-facing, chancel wall of a church, here with an arched canopy.

Scanned from: Parker, John Henry. *ABC of Gothic Architecture.* London: James Parker and Co, 1900, p. 129.

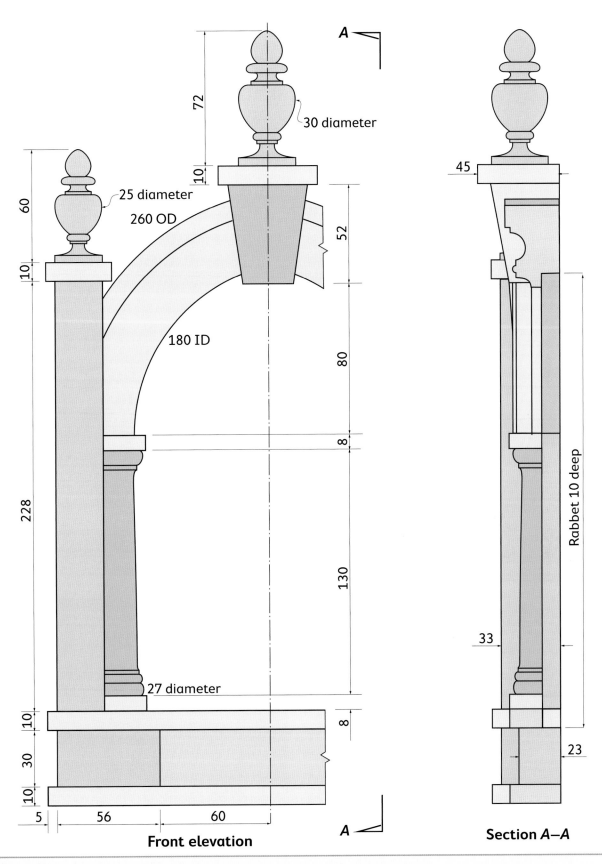

Figure 7.80 The design of the frame shown in figure 7.78 drawn half size.

7.10 FRAMES CONSTRUCTED FROM MORE THAN ONE ANNULUS

The arches of the diptych frame and the Gothic frame discussed above were each cut from one annulus of turned moulding. Use pieces of turned moulding cut from more than one annulus and the possibilities are immense as figures 7.82 and 7.83 suggest.

As figure 7.84 shows, when the ends of mouldings with the same cross section join, those ends aren't necessarily flat.

Figure 7.82 Although the top rail of this frame in the Scottish National Gallery in Edinburgh was probably carved in one piece, it could have been constructed from three pieces of turned moulding cut from two annular mouldings.

Figure 7.81 Frames in the Gothic style in the Scottish National Gallery in Edinburgh.

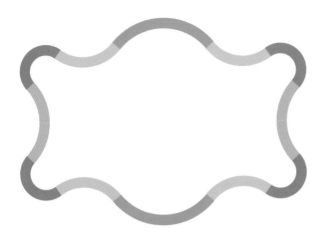

Figure 7.83 A frame made by dowelling together arcs from from four annular mouldings with the same cross section—however in two annular mouldings the cross section is transposed so that the rabbet is along the outer edge.

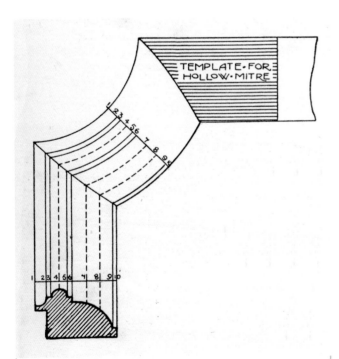

Figure 7.84 The curved intersection of a straight and a curved moulding.
Scanned from: Wells, Percy A. and Hooper, John. *Modern Cabinet Work Furniture & Fitments.* London: B. T. Batsford, 1909, p. 237.

7.11   ENDNOTES

1. Holtzapffel, John Jacob. Hand or Simple Turning. New York: Dover Publications, 1976, pp. 534 and 535. (Originally published in 1881.)

2. Scanned from: Kirby, Mary and Elizabeth. *Talks about Trees.* London: Casell, Petter, & Gilpin, undated but probably c. 1900, p. 309.

3. Walkling, Gillian. *Antique Bamboo Furniture.* London: Bell & Hyman, 1979, p.49.

4. Chippendale, Thomas. *The Gentlemen & Cabinet-Maker's Director.* New York: Dover Publications, 1966, plate XXVII. (Originally published in London in 1762.)

5. Serlio, Sebastiano. *The Five Books of Architecture.* New York: Dover Publications, 1982, third Booke folio 60. (Originally published in 1611.)

6. Palladio, Andrea. *The Four Books of Architecture,* New York: Dover Publications, 1965, plate XIII. (Originally published in 1738.)

Chapter 8

FUNNELS

Funnels are simple to turn, and attractive and functional. In this chapter I discuss them and describe how to make them.

One would expect *funnel*, *runnel*, *tunnel* and even the recent *Chunnel* (the rail tunnel beneath the English Channel) to all share some strong etymological connection, but their entries in the *OED* suggest that this is not so. On page 394 of his book *Treen and Other Wooden Bygones* Edward Pinto reminds us that brewers' funnels were sometimes called *tunnels*, and that a barrel was a *tun*. In late medieval times the size of a ship was measured by how many tuns of wine it could carry. Hence the terms *ton* and *tonnage*. However the word funnel is derived from the Latin *infundibulum* and the French *infundère*.

As figure 8.1 demonstrates, funnels have been made from metal, glass, plastic and ceramic materials, but before the Industrial Revolution most were made of wood. Multiple examples are shown in books by Pinto Evan-Thomas and Levi.[1, 2, 3] Antique funnels are therefore usually inexpensive, but as figure 8.2 shows, not always.

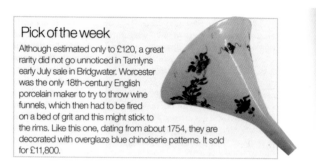

Figure 8.2 A report on the auction sale of an antique porcelain funnel scanned with permission from the August 7 2013 *Country Life* magazine.

8.1 FUNNEL DESIGN

Figures 8.3 and 8.4 show the three most common forms of wooden funnel. You can of course design funnels of particular sizes and for particular uses as figure 9.5 demonstrates. Funnel stem holes are usually tapered, but if the funnel is intended for pouring dry materials, there seems to be little point in facilitating a blockage some way down the stem.

Figure 8.1 Funnels made from, *left to right*: enamelled steel, plastic, glass, and wood (here London plane (*Platanus acerifolia*).

Figure 8.3 The three most common funnel forms. Funnels with bulbs, *left*, usually contained a wire mesh strainer.

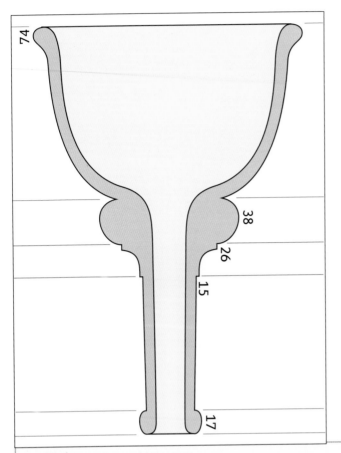

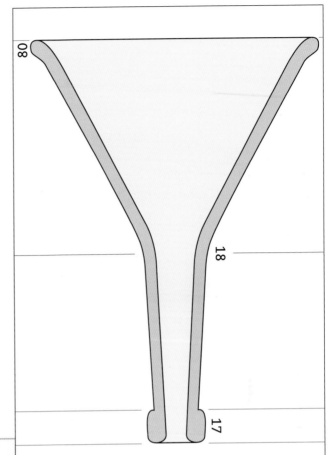

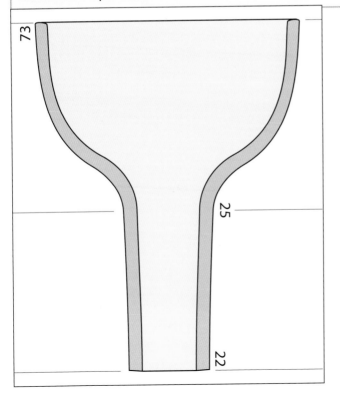

Figure 8.4 Pencil gauges for the three funnel forms shown in figure 9.3. You may want to scale these forms up or down.

Figure 8.5 A funnel (here cut in half) designed for filling a jar with screws and similar.

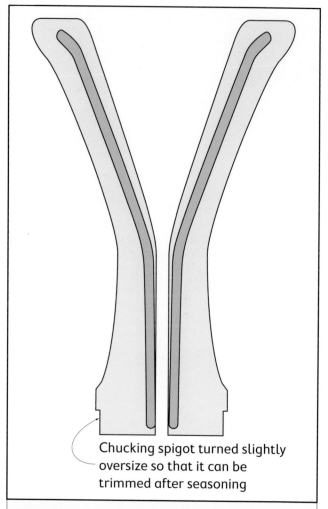

Chucking spigot turned slightly oversize so that it can be trimmed after seasoning

Figure 8.6 How to rough-turn a funnel work-piece prior to seasoning and finish-turning. Because the wood will shrink inwards, the bulk of the waste is left outside the intended finished form of the funnel.

8.2   MAKING FUNNELS

You can make funnels from one piece of seasoned wood, or you can turn the bowl and stem from separate work-pieces and glue or screw them together. You can also use unseasoned wood blanks; even those which include the pith if you chuck the workpiece for turning its pith coincident with the lathe axis.

A funnel workpiece should cut about 20-mm longer than the finished length of the funnel to allow for the bulb end to be flattened and for chucking. If using an unseasoned workpiece, you can rough-turn the funnel as in figure 8.6, and then allow it to season. Alternatively after rough-turning (including hollowing and boring), allow the workpiece to season and then finish-turn it. This procedure was used for the funnel shown being made in figures 8.7 to 8.17. Because the pith region was bored away and the funnel walls aren't too thick and can therefore warp during seasoning, cracking is unlikely although there will be some shrinkage.

Figure 8.7 Roughing the outside of an un-seasoned length of trunk. The driving and tail centers are located into the trunk's pith. At the workpiece's right-hand end I've already turned a chucking spigot. My pencil gauge for the funnel is shown on the bench behind.

Figure 8.9 Hollowing the bowl using a spindle detail gouge with its flute facing about 45° above the horizontal. The workpiece's chucking spigot is still held in the scroll chuck.

Figure 8.8 The workpiece has been trans-posed, and is being held by its chucking spigot in a scroll chuck at its left-hand end in a scroll chuck. Although the workpiece is cantilevered from the scroll chuck, for added security during roughing the tail center is supporting the work-piece's right-hand. I'm using the leading edge of a roughing gouge as a parting tool to roughly flatten the right-hand end.

Figure 8.10 Boring the axial stem hole (this drill has a Morse taper shank). I usually do this after hollowing the bulb, but the reverse is fine. After roughing is completed I put the workpiece aside for several weeks to season.

Figure 8.11   I've rechucked the now-seasoned workpiece. I'm first finish-turning the outside of the bowl.

Figure 8.13   Here while finish-turning the outside of the bowl, I'm monitoring the bowl's wall thickness with homemade callipers designed to measure wall thickness in restricted locations.

Figure 8.12   Finish-turning the inside of the funnel's bulb with a detail gouge.

Figure 8.14   If necessary rebore the stem hole. Then, if required, ream the stem hole to the desired taper. The reamer is made from the stem of a hand auger. I hacksawed a diagonal cut, and levered the cutting edge thus produced outwards so that it was a little proud. To widen the stem hole pull the reamer out to the right repeatedly.

Figure 8.15   A simple device to sand the inside surface of the stem. A small piece of abrasive cloth is gripped in a sawn slot in a piece of dowel. After sanding the outside and the inside of the bowl and the surface of the stem hole, the next operation is to turn the outside of the stem between centers.

Figure 8.16   I've turned a groove in a waste disk held on a screwchuck. The annular groove was sized to locate the wide end of the funnel. The bottom end of the stem hole will be located by the conical nose of a live tail center.

Figure 8.17   Finish-turning the outside of the stem. After sanding, the funnel is ready for any polishing.

8.3   ENDNOTES

1. Pinto, Edward H. *Treen and Other Wooden Bygones.* London: G. Bell & Sons, 1969, plates 9K, 136F and 423C.

2. Evan-Thomas, Owen. *Domestic Utensils of Wood.* London: Owen Evan-Thomas, 1932, plate 61.

3. Levi, Jonathan. *Treen for the Table.* Woodbridge, Suffolk: Antique Collectors' Club, 1998, p. 177.

Chapter 9

MARKERS

A bookmark is a strip of leather, card, cloth or other material inserted between two pages of a book to indicate where the reader wants to resume reading or where there is some content of note. I use card strips cut from breakfast cereal packets, and on the blank side write words that I see in the text which I need to look up in a dictionary (figure 9.1).

Book marker is a term which may be unfamiliar. It was to me until I came across an entry for a pair of antique book markers valued in 2003 at £800 to £1,000— figure 10.2 shows my replica. Thus *book marker* is not a synonym for *bookmark*, but refers to a marker that's used not between pages, but between books. When you remove a book from a shelf of books, the adjacent books typically tilt, and eventually distort. To prevent this, and enable you to quickly put the removed book back into its correct location, you could temporarily substitute a book marker for the removed book as shown in figure 9.3.

The high value for the antique pair confirms that book markers are rare objects: they're also useful, and are therefore a fitting subject for this book. Their concept can also be applied to other objects of similar shape to books which are kept in long lines on shelves such as CDs (figure 9.4) and DVDs (figure 9.5).

Figure 9.2 A replica of the pair of book markers shown in: Miller, Judith. *Collectables Price Guide 2003*. London: Dorling Kindersley, 2003, p. 533. The total length of each is 267 mm.

Figure 9.3 Using a book marker.

Figure 9.1 Card bookmarks and a 300-mm-long steel bar of square, 20 x 20 mm, cross section which I use to hold books open.

Figure 9.4 CD markers. That on the left has a chamfered leading edge. The spine of the plywood body on the right is veneered. The size of a plastic CD box is 142 x 125 x 10 mm.

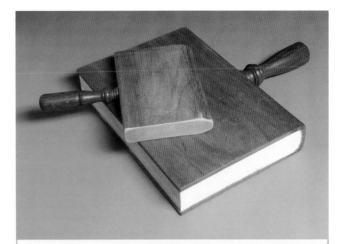

Figure 9.6 Two book markers. The size of the body of the upper marker is 107 x 150 x 21 mm. The body of the lower marker was made to resemble a book. Because of its large size (180 x 255 x 42 mm), to reduce its weight the body is constructed as a box.

Figure 9.5 DVD markers. The size of a plastic DVD box is 135 x 190 x 15 mm.

Book, CD and DVD markers are easy to make, and useful. And you can be almost certain that anyone who receives one won't already have any.

9.1 DESIGNING MARKERS

A marker is essentially a body in the form of a right rectangular prism with a handle projecting from the center of what might be called the body's *spine edge*. Chamfering the leading edge will make inserting the marker easier.

The design of the antique book markers is shown in figures 9.6 and 9.7. Figure 9.6 shows book markers with shorter handles (those of the antique markers are surely too long) and larger bodies. However without affecting their efficiency, the bodies of book markers can be made about two thirds of the height of the books they'll be used to mark. Large bodies are best made hollow like boxes or drilled so that they're not too heavy.

I make the bodies of markers for CDs and DVDs the same size as their respective plastic cases. The bodies can be cut from solid wood, or from plywood or another type of manufactured board. To improve the appearance of the CD marker with the plywood body shown in figure 9.6, I veneered its spine. Figures 9.9 to 9.11 show handles for DVD and CD markers.

Whether the bodies of antique book markers were always ornamented and decorated to resemble books I can't say. The "page edges" of the antique pair were gilt, not painted as in my replica.

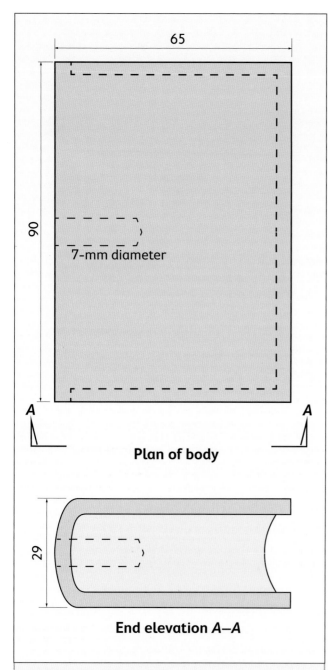

Figure 9.7   The design of the bodies of the book markers shown in figure 9.2.

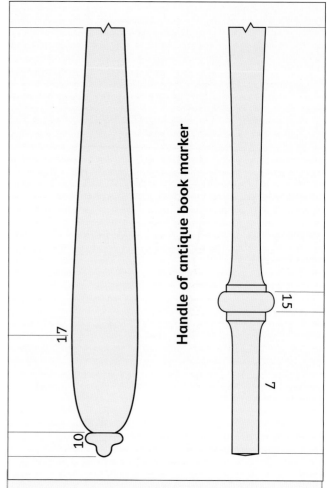

Figure 9.8   A pencil gauge for the handles of the book markers shown in figure 9.2.

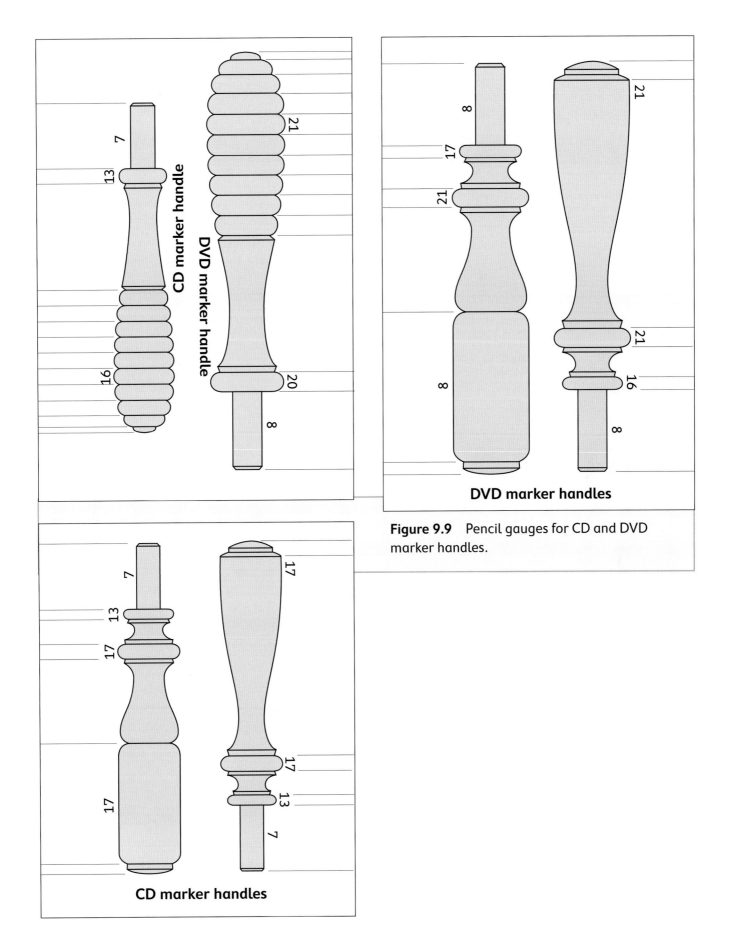

CD marker handle

DVD marker handle

DVD marker handles

Figure 9.9   Pencil gauges for CD and DVD marker handles.

CD marker handles

9.2   MAKING MARKERS

I turn marker handles between centers with their pins to the right. As shown in figure 9.10, I then chuck each handle by its pin for finish-turning and polishing.

Handles for markers are usually located halfway up the spine. When drilling the spine for the handle's pin, if the body is thin, clamp the body across where it's being drilled so that it won't split during the drilling.

Figure 9.10   Holding a marker's handle by its pin to finish-turn its right-hand end. This chucking method is also ideal to use for polishing operations.

Chapter 10

MOLINILLOS

A ceramic pot with a hole in the lid similar to that on the left of figure 10.1, or a silver pot with a hole in the lid covered by its own smaller lid similar to that in figure 10.2, isn't a coffee pot, it's a chocolate pot.

Until the late 19th century most chocolate was consumed in drinks. However chocolate mixes poorly with water. To overcome this the molinillo was invented in Spain in the late 16th century. By rapidly rubbing your palms and fingers to and fro with the molinillo's shaft located between them as shown in figure 10.3, you create a manual version of a milkshake machine, and thus froth and better mix the chocolate into the solution. Hence the French call a molinillo a *moussoir* meaning 'froth-maker'.

Why would you want to make a molinillo? One reason is because most chocolate pots have not retained

Figure 10.1 *Left*, a 21st-century chocolate pot made by BIA Cordon Bleu; *rear center*, a brand of drinking chocolate (a powder consisting of cocoa presscake combined with milk); *rear right*, a brand of cocoa powder (powdered cocoa presscake); and *front*, three molinillos. The rear molinillo was supplied with the chocolate pot. I made the front and central molinillos. The front molinillo has seven V-cuts and six valleys, the central one has four valleys.

their original molinillo. Also a molinillo can also be used to froth a chocolate drink in less specific vessels.

This chapter describes how to make a molinillo, but before doing so introduces the source, the history and the manufacture of chocolate. I've found the four books listed in the endnotes invaluable in writing this content.

Figure 10.3 Frothing drinking chocolate in hot milk with a molinillo.

Figure 10.2 A 23.5-cm-high silver chocolate pot made in Paris in 1766 by François Thomas Germain. The handle at right angles to the spout was a French innovation. The French term for chocolate pot is *chocolatière*.

In the collection of the Metropolitan Museum of Art, New York. Photograph sourced from Wikimedia Commons.

10.1   THE CHOCOLATE TREE

The *Theobroma* (meaning 'food of the gods') genus of trees has 22 species. Only the seeds (usually called *beans* because of their large size) of *Theobroma cocoa* can be used to produce chocolate. An understory tree, it's native to the lush tropical rainforests of Mesoamerica and South America (figure 10.4). Carl Linnaeus, gave the tree its botanic name in 1753 after receiving details of the tree from Sir Hans Sloane (of whom more later).

There are three main varieties of chocolate tree: *criollo*, *forastero*, and *trinitario* (a hybrid of the first two which appeared in Trinidad). The *criollo* variety produces the finest chocolate and is native to the tropical rainforests of Mesoamerica. Only about 2% of the world crop is of this variety, and it's reserved for the finest chocolate. The *forastero* variety is native to the north and west of the Amazon basin and the coastal rainforests of Equador; is a more robust and higher-yielding variety than the criollo, but the resulting chocolate has a poorer flavor. 80% of the current production of cocoa beans is sourced from *forastero* trees grown throughout the tropics, especially in west Africa.

The flowers of *Theobroma* trees are pollinated by midges which breed in the decaying vegetable matter on on the forest floor. About six months after flowering, the large pods are ready to harvest (figure 10.5). Each pod is 15 to 30 centimeters long, and yields 30 to 40 almond-shaped seeds surrounded by a sweet white pulp figure 10.6). In the wild, monkeys break open the pods to get at the pulp, thus scattering the seeds which have an unpleasant bitter taste.

Figure 10.5   Cocoa pods on a chocolate tree of the forastero variety.
Sourced from Wikimedia Commons.

Figure 10.4   *Right*, the first European illustration of a chocolate tree appeared in *Historia del Mondo Nuovo* [History of the New World] published in Venice in 1565 by Girolamo Benzoni. Benzoni (1519–1572) travelled widely in the New World between 1541 and 1556.

This image scanned from page 43 of the Dover Publications edition of *Medicinal and Food Plants* by Ernst and Johanna Lehner.

Figure 10.6   Cocoa pods split to show their beans encased in a white pulp.
Sourced from Wikimedia Commons.

10.2 EARLY USES OF CHOCOLATE

Raw cocoa beans are bitter. It's believed that the first people to process cocoa beans to decrease that bitterness, release the chocolate flavor, and thus allow the creation of a palatable drink were the Mesoamerican Olmec who flourished between 1500 and 400 BC. Later empires, notably the Maya, the Toltecs, and the Aztecs, processed the beans similarly using the first six steps in figure 10.7. These are:

1. fermentation which requires five to six days. During this the seeds germinate briefly before being killed by the high temperature and acidity, and the pulp liquefies and drains away

2. drying which takes one to two weeks if done in the open

3. roasting for between 70 and 115 minutes at between 100 °C and 120 °C. After roasting the beans have darkened, lost over half their weight, and lost their bitter taste because of the complex chemical changes which have taken place

4. winnowing to remove the seed shells

5. chopping the roasted, de-shelled beans into small pieces called *nibs*

6. grinding the nibs on a heated plate called a *metate*, (figure 10.8).

The indians then mixed the paste left after grinding (now called *cocoa mass*) with water and with other ingredients including maize, chilli, and vanilla, to create a chocolate drink. To increase this drink's palatability and to create a froth or foam, this broth was poured from one pot to another. An alternative method was to shake the broth in a screw-topped pottery container—perhaps the earliest application of a screwed lid? The Spanish however eschewed such crude methods and invented the molinillo.

The first recorded European contact with chocolate was on 15 August 1502. During Columbus's fourth trip to the New World, his men captured two Mayan trading canoes whose cargoes included strange-looking "almonds".

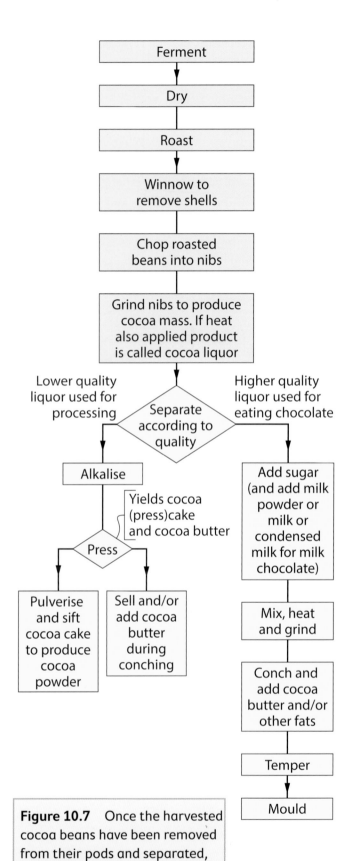

Figure 10.7 Once the harvested cocoa beans have been removed from their pods and separated, they are processed as described in this flow chart.

Figure 10.8   Grinding cocoa nibs on a heated metate. From Nicolas de Blégny's 1687 treatise Le bon usage du thé, du caffé, et du chocolat.
From the Welcome Trust, Welcome Images. Sourced from Wikimedia Commons

Figure 10.9   The mancerina, a galleried saucer, was invented by the gallant Marquez de Mancera in Peru in about 1640 to prevent chocolate drinks being spilled and thus staining the sumptuous clothing worn then by those who could afford the drink. The equivalent French term is *trembleuse*. This hard-paste porcelain trembleur was manufactured by the Du Paquier factory in Vienna between 1735 and 1740.
In the collection of the Gardiner Museum, Toronto. Sourced from Wikimedia Commons.

The Spanish invasion and conquest of Mesoamerica and South America began in 1519. The first documented use of chocolate in Europe was in Spain in 1544. Chocolate reached England in the 1550s and north America by the beginning of the 18th century, but but its consumption was restricted to the wealthy until late into the 19th century. This consumption was primarily in the form of a drink, and to lessen the probability of spillage staining expensive clothing the mancerina was introduced (figure 10.9).

10.3   MODERN PROCESSING

Today there are three main, distinct, chocolate products: coca powder, dark chocolate, and milk chocolate. The processings listed in the yellow boxes of figure 10.7 necessary to produce these products with the qualities we now know and love and in the desired quantities and at affordable prices weren't invented until the 19th century.

The six steps listed in the blue boxes in figure 10.7 are still necessary irrespective of which chocolate product is to be produced. Step 6, grinding the nibs, produces cocoa mass, a thick paste which contains cocoa solids and about 55% by weight of the fat cocoa butter. Cocoa butter melts at between 34 °C and 38 °C. Gently heating cocoa mass converts it into cocoa liquor, also called chocolate liquor. If cocoa liquor is cooled it becomes unsweetened, gritty, solid chocolate.

Adding sugar (which is produced from cane {native to India} or beet {native to Silesia}) to counteract the remaining bitterness was introduced shortly after the Spanish started to consume chocolate.

In 1815 Dutch chemist Casparus van Houten (1770–1858) investigated the Aztec practice of adding wood ash to the ground nibs. He treated cocoa liquor with the alkaline salts potassium and sodium carbonate. This

'Dutching' process improved the flavor, darkened the color, and improved miscibility.

Swiss chocolatier Philippe Suchard (1797–1874) in about 1826 invented the world's first mélangeur or mixing-and-grinding machine (figure 10.10). This greatly speeded both grinding and the incorporation into the chocolate liquor of such as alkalizing componds, sugar, and, for milk chocolate, milk powder.

In 1828 Coenraad Van Houten (figure 10.11) , son of Casparus, developed a hydraulic press which squeezed the cocoa liquor and thus reduced its cocoa butter content from 55% to about 27% by weight. Before then the content of cocoa butter in cocoa mass could only be slightly reduced by heating the cocoa mass and skimming the cocoa butter from the top of the cocoa liquor. The press cake left after the hydraulic pressing was then able to be pulverised, unlike the cocoa butter-rich nibs.

In 1847 J.S. Fry & Sons of Bristol found a way to produce somewhat gritty chocolate bars by pouring a heated blend of cocoa powder, sugar and melted cocoa butter into moulds. As the blend cooled, it set.

Figure 10.11   Coenraad Van Houten (1801–1887),
Sourced from Wkimedia Commons.

Figure 10.10   A mélangeur similar to that invented by Philippe Suchard in use at the Ghirardelli Chocolate Company in San Francisco. The giant granite rollers crush the cocoa nibs and sugar against the heated bed to produce first an oily paste and then a thick liquid.
Illustration courtesy of Flickr.

The grittiness problem was solved in 1879 when Rodolphe Lindt in Berne invented the agitating, crushing and aerating process called conching (figures 10.12 and 10.13). After about three days of continuous conching, the cocoa particle diameters are reduced to about 25 microns (diameters above 50 microns feel gritty).

The association of chocolate with milk may have started in England.

I mentioned Sir Hans Sloane earlier (figure 10.14). Although Sloane Square, the habitat of the eponymous rangers, is perhaps his best-known memorial, Sloane was a physician, scientist (president of the Royal Society from 1727 to 1740) and collector. (On Sloane's death the nation bought his collection, and it became the base collection for the British Museum.) In 1688 Sloane, then a physician, had accompanied the new governor of Jamaica to the island. There Sloane was introduced to the drink of chocolate mixed with water. Finding it nauseous, and decided to try mixing the chocolate with

Figure 10.12   Rodolphe Lindt (1855–1909).
Courtesy Lindt & Sprungli.

Figure 10.14   Sir Hans Sloane (1660–1753).
Sourced from Wikimedia Commons.

Figure 10.13   A conch similar to that invented
by Lindt. The heavy roller is driven to and
fro along the heated bed of the conche. This
rolling and the slapping of the liquor against
the upcurved ends of the conche bed reduces
the cocoa's particle size, enables the addition
of extra cocoa butter, and allows the resulting
liquor to be readily moulded.
Courtesy Zum Wald, Switzerland.

hot milk instead. By 1727 Nicholas Sanders, a grocer in London's Soho, was selling a medicinal elixir based on Sloane's recipe called 'Sir Hans Sloan's Milk Chocolate'.

But solid milk chocolate wasn't produced until 1879. Henri Nestlé, (figure 10.15) a Swiss chemist had by 1867 developed a process to make powdered milk by evaporation. Swiss chocolate manufacturer Daniel Peter (figure 10.16), a neighbor of Nestlé in Vevey, Switzerland, then experimented adding cocoa butter and Nestlé's milk powder to cocoa powder. In 1879 he produced the first bars of milk chocolate.

Today there is a range of qualities of chocolate. The highest quality results from the use of criollo beans, extended conching, and cocoa butter instead of cheaper fats. Chocolate is sometimes labelled with a percentage of chocolate. The remaining percentage consists of compounds, chiefly sugar, not sourced from cocoa beans.

Figure 10.16   Daniel Peter (1836–1919). Illustration courtesy of Nestlé Historical Archives, Vevey.

10.4 MAKING A MOLINILLO

A molinillo consists of a shaft, and a head which is designed to agitate the chocolate and milk or water mixture. When the molinillo is intended to be used with a lidded chocolate pot, the maximum diameter of the molinillo's shaft is limited by the size of the hole in the pot's lid. I experimented with locally increasing and decreasing the shaft diameter where it's between the hands, but there didn't seem to be any resulting benefit.

Design
Figures 10.17 and 10.18 show the design of the front molinillo pictured in figure 10.1. That molinillo's head is similar to ones shown in a 1687 French treatise by Nicolas de Blegny,[5] and in 17th- and 18th-century still-life paintings. Molinillos can be turned in one piece or two.

Figure 10.15   Henri Nestlé (1814–1890 in 1867. Illustration courtesy of Nestlé Historical Archives, Vevey.

Making

I have seen antique molinillos in ebony and in beech. For the two molinillos shown in the front of figure 10.1 I used ash (*Fraxinus excelsior*) for the heads and beech (*Fagus sylvatica*) for the shafts. How to make the molinillo shown in the front of figure 10.1 is shown in figures 10.19 to 10.26.

Although molinillos weren't usually polished, you could apply a nontoxic finish.

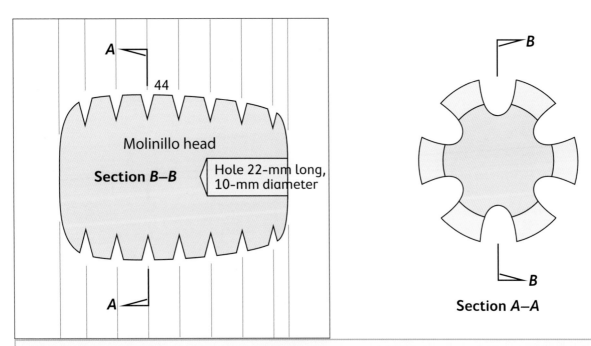

Figure 10.17   A pencil gauge and cross section for the head of the front molinillo in figure 10.1.

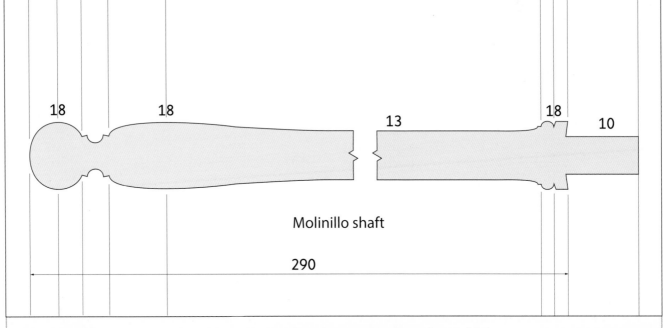

Figure 10.18   A pencil gauge for the shaft of the front molinillo in figure 10.1.

Figure 10.19   Boring the 10-mm-diameter hole for the shaft pin into the head's workpiece which is cantilevered from a scroll chuck. The blue tape on the drill is a hole depth guide.

Figure 10.20   The head has been turned to its final profile, bored, and is here being marked out. My lathe's indexing facility has 24 holes. To draw the twelve equally spaced horizontal lines, I made a horizontal platform which fits into the lathe's banjo. The top of the platform is at the height of the lathe axis less half the the thickness of the pencil.

Figure 10.21   V-cutting the V-grooves with a skew's long point.

Figure 10.22   Carving one of the six longitudinal valleys.

Figure 10.23 After sanding, parting-off the head with a skew's long point.

Figure 10.25 Sanding the head's right-hand end after finish-turning it.

Figure 10.26 Turning the molinillo's shaft. Here I'm planing from left to right.

Figure 10.24 Reverse-chucking the head on a 10-mm-diameter pin turned in a piece of waste wood.

10.5 ENDNOTES

1. Cadbury, D. *Chocolate Wars*. London: Harper Press, 2010.

2. Clarence-Smith, William Gervase. *Cocoa and Chocolate, 1765–1914*. Abingdon: Routledge, 2000.

3. Coe, Sophie D. and Michel D. *The True History of Chocolate*. London: Thames & Hudson, 1996.

4. McFadden, C. and France, C. *The Ultimate Encyclopedia of Chocolate*. London: Lorenz Books, 1997.

5. Coe, Sophie D. and Michel D. *The True History of Chocolate*. London: Thames & Hudson, 1996, pp. 116 and 117.

MONAURAL STETHOSCOPES

What gift could you turn for a medical student, medical practitioner, midwife or father to be? How about a monaural stethoscope? This chapter introduces stethoscopes and describes how to turn the version shown in figure 11.1.

11.1 HISTORY OF THE STETHOSCOPE

The term *stethoscope* derives from the Greek words for chest (stēthos) and for examination (scopos). A *stetho-*

Figure 11.1   Two Robertson-design monaural stethoscopes turned in ash, *Fraxinus excelsior*, and copied from the original in the collection of Berrima District Museum in the Southern Highlands of New South Wales, Australia.

scope is thus 'an instrument used for examining the chest or other part of the body by auscultation (the act of listening to the sounds within the body to form a diagnosis). Hippocrates in the fourth century B.C. had described the splashing noise which could be heard on shaking a patient who had pus in his chest. Auscultation was then neglected until 1761 when the Viennese physician Leopold Auenbrugger published his treatise *Inventum Novum* (New Discovery) on percussion of the chest. Auenbrugger was an innkeeper's son who applied his early experience of thumping barrels to test their fullness to diagnosis. By tapping with a finger of one hand onto one of the fingers of the other hand placed in contact with the patient's body, the physician could determine the size of organs in the body and establish the presence of an abnormal internal collection of gas or fluid.[1]

Early in the nineteenth century physicians began to study bodily sounds such as those produced in the lungs by breathing and by the heart beating. For this the physician placed his (there weren't any female physicians) ear on the patient's skin over the subject organ. This is called *immediate auscultation*.

It wasn't then long before the more effective mediate (acting through an intermediate agency) auscultation was introduced. The Parisian physician René Théophile Hyacinthe Laënnec (figure 11.2) was a shy person who in 1816 invented the monaural (for one ear) stethoscope to avoid the embarassment of having to put his ear against the chests of his female patients. His first stethoscope, derived from an ear trumpet (figure 11.3), was a sheaf of papers rolled into a cylinder. Figures 11.4 and 11.5 show improved monaural stethoscopes designed by Laennec.[2]

A binaural (for both ears) stethoscope was developed using flexible lead tubing in 1829. Later versions used tubing formed from coiled metal covered in fabric. In 1855 the first commercially-successful binaural stethoscope started to be commercially produced. It had been designed by Dr Cammann of New York, and featured rubber tubing.[3] Some modern stethoscopes now feature electronic sound volume amplification.

In 1895 in Paris Adolphe Pinard (figure 11.6) introduced a form of monaural stethoscope for listening to foetal heartbeats.[3] The trumpet-shaped end of a Pinard horn which is placed against the mother's body (figure 11.7) is larger in maximum diameter than that of most monaural stethoscopes. The Pinard horn is still in use today, particularly by midwives.

Figure 11.2   René-Théophile-Hyacinthe Laennec (1781–1826). He also introduced the medical terms *cirrhosis* and *melanoma*. *Cirrhosis* is derived from the Greek word *kirrhos* for the color tawny which is the color of the nodules which form on the liver as the disease worsens. *Melanoma* is derived from the Greek *mela*, meaning 'black', the color of the cancerous cells which form on the skin.
    Sourced from Wikimedia commons.

Figure 11.3   A nineteenth-century, metal, telescopic ear trumpet made in London. Ear trumpets had been in use since at least the start of the 16th century.
    Sourced from Wellcome Images.

Figure 11.4   A monaural stethoscope once owned by René Laennec.
    Sourced from Wellcome Images.

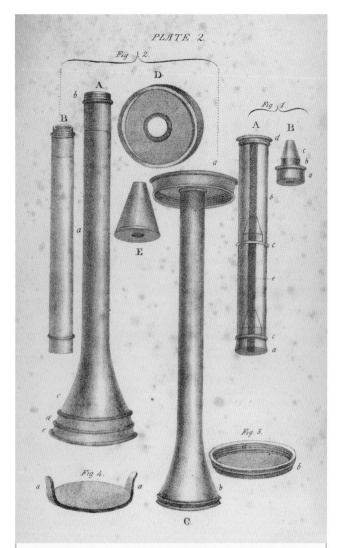

Figure 11.5 Monaural stethoscopes shown in the frontispiece to Laennec's 1819 book. Its title translated into English is: *On Mediate Ausculation or Treatise on the Diagnosis of the Diseases of the Lungs and Heart*.

Sourced from Wellcome Images.

Figure 11.6 Adolphe Pinard (1844–1934), French obstetrician. The Boulevard Adolphe-Pinard in Paris is a reminder of his services to obstetrics.

Sourced from Wellcome Images.

Figure 11.7 A Pinard foetal stethoscope or horn made in London early in the 20th century, and used to listen to the foetus within the womb. The medical professional puts his or her ear to the lower end.

Sourced from Wellcome Images.

11.2 MAKING A MONAURAL STETHOSCOPE

The original of the stethoscope shown in figure 11.1 was turned in ebony, but any fine-grained hardwood will do for a replica. I used a 3/16-inch {4.76-mm} -diameter long series twist drill to bore the through hole. As in many monaural stethoscopes the through hole's diameter is substantially greater, this diameter wouldn't seem to be critical.

11.2.1 Turning the base

Figure 11.8 shows a gauge for the base. The recommended procedure is:

1. Prepare a base workpiece, a disk with transverse grain, and bore the 10-mm-diameter through hole.

2. Turn a mandrel of about 10-mm diameter on which the workpiece can be chucked by friction between the mandrel and the surface of the 10-mm-diameter hole (figure 11.9).

3. Mount the disk on the 10-mm-diameter mandrel, and gently finish-turn and sand the bottom of the base (figure 11.10).

4. Transpose the disk on the mandrel (figure 12.11) and finish-turn and sand the top surface of the base (figure 11.12).

Figure 11.9　A 10-mm-diameter mandrel.

Figure 12.10　Turning the bottom of the base with a detail gauge.

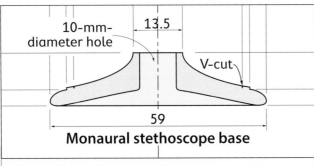

Figure 11.8　A pencil gauge for the stethoscope base.

Figure 11.11　About to rechuck the base workpiece on the mandrel to finish-turn the base's top surface.

Figure 11.12 Turning the top of the base with a detail gouge.

11.2.2 Turning the stem

The procedure you adopt to turn the stem will depend on whether you have a drill long enough to bore through the stem's whole length, or whether you need to bore from both ends. Another variable is the chuck you decide to use to hold the workpiece for boring and belling. The steps are:

1. Prepare for the stem an axially-grained workpiece a couple of millimetres longer than the stem's finished length, and large enough in cross section to allow a 30-mm-diameter cylinder to be turned from it. Also depending on how the end(s) of the workpiece need to be turned for chucking

2. Punch centering recesses in both ends so that the workpiece will have its grain exactly axial when mounted between centers.

3. Rough the stem workpiece to a cylinder of 30-mm diameter or bigger between centers, and cut the right-hand end flat with a skew's long point (figure 11.14). Mark the stem's finished length at its left-hand end (figure 11.15).

4. Chuck the stem axially by what was its right-hand end (figure 11.16).

5. Trim the workpiece's right-hand end back to the stem's finished length with a skew's long point.

6. Bore the stem workpiece halfway (figure 11.17). Unfortunately there's no such thing as a self-centering drill.

7. Bell the ear end of the stem (figure 11.18).

8. Finish-turn the outside of the bell (figure 11.19) and sand the bell's inside and outside.

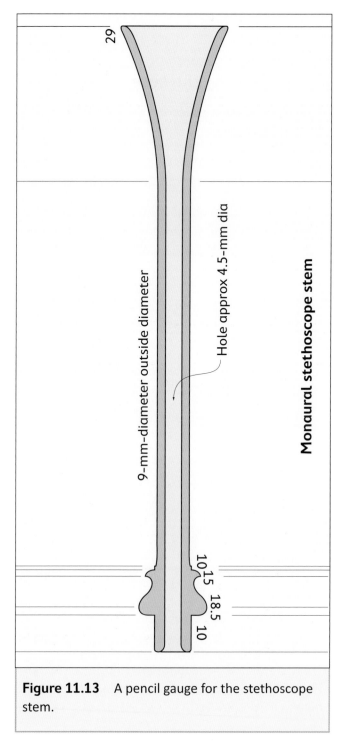

Figure 11.13 A pencil gauge for the stethoscope stem.

Figure 11.14 Flattening the right-hand end of the stem workpiece with a skew's long point. I'm using the tied-underhand grip, and pushing the skew bodily forwards in an arc with the left hand in charge.

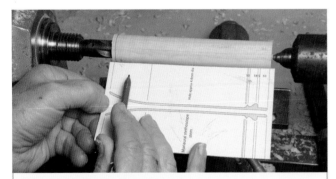

Figure 11.15 Marking the finished length at the workpiece's left-hand end.

Figure 11.16 Truing the rotation of the workpiece by levering up its right-hand end. The chuck is fairly, but not fully, tightened.

9. Chuck the belled end in a press fit chuck (figure 11.20).

10. Finish-turn and sand the rest of the stem's outside surface.

11. Polish the components as required. To sand between coats, it's best the rechuck the two parts.

12. Glue the stem into the base.

Figure 11.17 Boring, here with an extra long 3/16-inch-diameter twist drill. To creat a truly axial starting recess, I used a skew's long point. Run the lathe fairly fast, say at 1500 rpm or faster. If shavings build up in the bored hole, the drill is more likely to wander. Therefore withdraw and clean the drill every 10 mm of hole depth.

Figure 11.18   Belling the ear end of the stem with a small detail gouge axially rotated about 45° anticlockwise. Small detail gouges are discussed on pages 13 to 16.

Figure 11.20   About to chuck the belled end of the stem workpiece into a press-fit chuck whose recess has been turned to grip the outside of the bell.

Figure 11.21   Finish-turning the remainder of the outside of the stem.

11.3   ENDNOTES

1. Porter, Roy. *The Greatest Benefit to Mankind*. London: Harper Collins, 1997, p. 256.

2. Porter, Roy. *The Greatest Benefit to Mankind*. London: Harper Collins, 1997, pp. 308–309.

3. Craughwell, Thomas J. *30,000 Years of Inventions*. New York: Tess Press, 2012, pp. 204–205.

Figure 11.19   Turning the outside of the bell with a detail gouge. You could support the workpiece's right-hand end with a live tail center having a conical nose, or a wooden cone which locates on the tail center's nose.

Chapter 12

A NEGUS STRAINER

"I love children, especially when they cry, for then someone takes them away." If, unlike Nancy Mitford, you don't have a "someone" on hand, there is still the eponymous solution invented by Colonel Francis Negus.

In this chapter I'll introduce Colonel Negus and his drink (not to be confused with a Negus, a hereditary ruler of Ethiopia). I'll then describe how to turn a negus strainer. Examples of these strainers are shown in figure 12.1 and at least four books.[1, 2, 3, 4] Negus strainers make excellent gifts because you can be almost certain that their recipients won't already have one.

12.1 COLONEL NEGUS

Colonel Francis Negus (1660–1732) served in the War of the Spanish Succession under John Churchill 1st Duke of Marlborough, attained the rank of lieutenant-colonel in the Suffolk regiment of foot, held various court and other English military appointments, and was an MP for Ipswitch from 1717 until his death at his home (figure 12.2) in the village of Dallinghoo, Suffolk, (figure 12.3)

Figure 12.2   Colonel Negus's home in its current enlarged state in Dallinghoo.

This photograph and other information about colonel Negus was generously supplied by Trevor Blackman, secretary of the Suffolk Mid-Coastal Woodturning Club which meets at Dallinghoo.

Figure 12.1   *Left*, a negus strainer with the typical shallow bowl turned in blackwood (*Acacia melanoxylon*); *right*, the mahogany (*Swietenia macrophylla*) strainer with a deeper bowl, the making of which is described in this chapter.

Figure 12.3   The location of Dallinghoo about 130 km northeast of London.
Sourced from Maps in Minutes.

on 9 September 1732. He is said to have invented negus sometime in the first quarter of the 18th century, evidently in an unsuccessful attempt to reduce intoxication at regimental dinners. (Negus at about 6.5% alcohol by volume is considerably less intoxicating than modern table wines.)

12.2   NEGUS

Negus was a popular drink in England outside the military during the second half of the 18th and throughout the 19th centuries. It was mentioned in novels by among others: Jane Austen, James Boswell, Charlotte Brontë, Emily Brontë, John Buchan, Arthur Conan Doyle, Charles Dickens, John Galsworthy, P.D. James, Patrick O'Brian, and William Makepiece Thackeray.

Negus's best-known recipe is in Mrs Beeton's famous book, an offshoot of her husband's *The Englishwoman's Domestic Magazine* started in 1852, and is shown in figure 12.4. Her book, perhaps anticipating Nancy Mitford's attitude, promoted negus as a children's party drink.

Mrs Beeton's recipe has imperial quantities. Below is a metric and slightly simpler version which assumes you use 750 ml (the usual capacity of a modern bottle) of port wine.

- Into a suitable jug or bowl put 150 gm of granulated or caster sugar and the rind, excluding any pith, of one or two lemons.
- Add 1.5 liters of boiling water.
- Stir the mixture to dissolve the sugar. Allow the mixture to steep for a short while.
- Add the ruby port and stir.
- Strain off the lemon rind while pouring the negus into glasses, and add nutmeg to taste. Alternatively strain the negus into a jug or punch bowl from which the negus can later be transferred into individual glasses. Nutmeg is then ground or powdered nutmeg is added into each glass to taste.

The port wine in the negus recipe is what today we would call *ruby port*. When making this wine, as the alcohol level of the fermenting must (grape juice, skins and seeds) reaches about 7% by volume, brandy

is added. This halts the fermentation. The young, fortified wine is then aged in cask for about eighteen months before bottling, and has a sweet, rich flavor.

Port was invented to overcome a shortage of French wine in Britain. During the 17th and 18th centuries shipping claret from Bordeaux was restricted because of the

> ### TO MAKE NEGUS.
>
> 1835. INGREDIENTS.—To every pint of port wine allow 1 quart of boiling water, ¼ lb. of sugar, 1 lemon, grated nutmeg to taste.
>
> *Mode.*—As this beverage is more usually drunk at children's parties than at any other, the wine need not be very old or expensive for the purpose, a new fruity wine answering very well for it. Put the wine into a jug, rub some lumps of sugar (equal to ¼ lb.) on the lemon-rind until all the yellow part of the skin is absorbed, then squeeze the juice, and strain it. Add the sugar and lemon-juice to the port wine, with the grated nutmeg; pour over it the boiling water, cover the jug, and, when the beverage has cooled a little, it will be fit for use. Negus may also be made of sherry, or any other sweet white wine, but is more usually made of port than of any other beverage.
>
> *Sufficient.*—Allow 1 pint of wine, with the other ingredients in proportion, for a party of 9 or 10 children.

Figure 12.4   The recipe for negus scanned from: Beeton, Isabella. *The Book of Household Management*. London: S. O. Beeton, 1861, p. 890.

Figure 13.5   A bottle of ruby port (formerly called *port wine*), a glass of negus, a lemon squeezer, lemon, nutmeg, and a negus strainer.

intermittent wars between England and France. English wine merchants looked to Portugal's Douro valley as an alternative wine source. Because of the longer voyage duration and higher temperatures experienced during it, it was necessary to add alcohol fortify the wine to prevent spoilage. The resulting wine is called *port* because Oporto or Porto was, and is, the shipping entrepot at the mouth of the Douro river.

12.3   MAKING A NEGUS STRAINER

Mrs Beeton's and other negus recipes specify that the lemon rind and any other solids be strained off. Antique negus strainers are wood rather than wire mesh although wire mesh had been in use for about 250 years by the 18th century, for example in paper making. Below I describe how I made the strainer with the deeper-than-usual bowl shown on the right-hand side of figure 12.1 and in figure 12.6. The strainer's form and dimensions however aren't critical.

Three problems have to be overcome:

1. turning a transversely grained object whose length is substantially greater than its breadth
2. minimising splintering around the strainer holes by drilling them before finish-turning the two surfaces through which they emerge
3. turning the inside of the strainer bowl which has a steep, slightly concave wall, and a tight radius connecting the wall to an only slightly concave bottom.

The strainer should be turned from a hardish, fine-grained wood. Such woods tend to be expensive and not readily available in wide planks. As figure 12.6 shows, the strainer's design features a much deeper bowl than usual to reduce the likelihood of the negus overflowing as it is being strained.

The strainer workpiece is a 200-mm-long plank with a cross section of 83 x 43 mm. To be able to turn the strainer "sweetly" I converted the workpiece into a disk by gluing on waste wood cheeks (radiata pine) as shown in figure 12.7. The steps were then:

- Mount the composite workpiece on a screwchuck or a faceplate, finish-turn the workpiece's periphery to 200-mm-diameter, and skim its right-hand face flat.
- The workpiece is too thick to be able to drill the 2-mm-diameter strainer holes from the workpiece's top. Therefore drill them into and through the workpiece's bottom face. To do this pencil the locations of the strainer holes as shown in figure 12.7.
- If you have screwed the workpiece onto a faceplate, before dechucking the workpiece make suitable marks so that you can rechuck the workpiece on the faceplate in the same orientation.
- Dechuck the workpiece from the screwchuck or faceplate. Using a bradawl point, impress the hole positions, and drill the holes about 10 mm deep (figure 12.8).
- Rechuck the workpiece as before. Finish-turn and sand the bowl's bottom and wings' undersides. Ensure that the wing' undersides are flat (figure 12.9).
- Dechuck the workpiece
- Screw a 200 mm diameter backing disk of plywood more than 12-mm-thick onto a faceplate. Turn a recess in the disk such that when the bottom of the strainer bowl is a snug fit within the recess the underside of the wings just contact the backing disk (figure 12.10).
- Drill two screw clearance holes through the backing disk and screw the workpiece to the backing disk as shown in figure 12.10.
- Finish-turn and sand the inside of the bowl. You'll need to unscrew the workpiece from the backing disk at least once to monitor progress (figures 12.11 to 12.16).
- Finish-turn the outside of the bowl above the wings (figure 12.17) and the top of the wings, but don't attempt to turn off the outer waste into which the two screws shown in figure 12.10 penetrate.
- Turn a shallow disk shown in figure 12.18 which fits snuggly against and within the rim of the strainer bowl.
- Force the live tail-center against the shallow disk, remove the two screws shown in figure 12.10, and start to turn off the outer waste (figure 12.18).

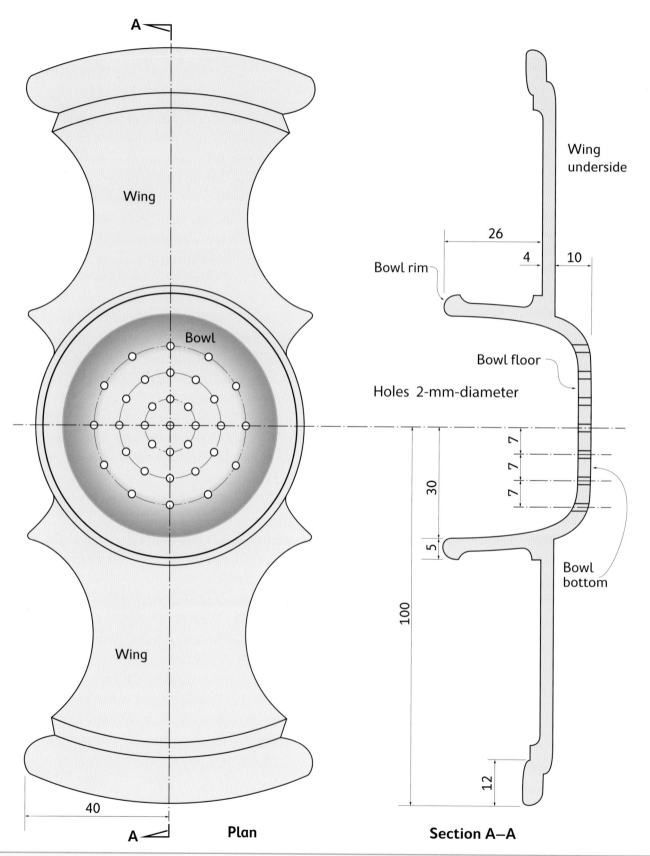

Figure 12.6 The negus strainer pictured on the right-hand side of figure 12.1.

- You may be able to finish-turn and sand the top surfaces of the wings with the workpiece just held by the tail center and shallow disk. There is a more secure way which prevents any wing flexing: once the the outer wings are close to their finished thickness, insert two screws with their heads well recessed through the outer parts of the waste cheeks and into the backing disk (figure 12.19). You can readily undo these two screws to dechuck the workpiece to monitor progress.
- Dechuck the finish-turned and sanded workpiece from the backing disk. Mark out the edges of the wings from a template (figure 12.20).
- Saw and/or carve and sand the edges of the wings (figure 12.21).
- Polishing is optional. Use a safe, oil-like finish. If you use a varnish or lacquer it's likely that the strainer holes will become clogged.
- Open the ruby port and make the negus.

Figure 12.8   Drilling the 2-mm-diameter strainer holes. I've previously pressed the point of the bradawl shown left into the strainer hole center marks to make it easier to accurately position the workpiece under the drill.

Figure 12.7   I've trued the periphery and flattened the right-hand face of the composite mahogany and pine workpiece. I've also pencilled the center of the workpiece, and the three circles and the six diameters on which the strainer hole centers lie. In addition I've made fine V-cuts with a skew's long point on the three circles to aid positioning the bradawl's point when impressing the hole positions.

Figure 12.9   I've finish-turned the bottom of the bowl and the underside of the wings. Here I'm checking that the wings are flat.

Figure 12.10   I've screwed a plywood backing disk onto a faceplate, and turned a hollow recess into that disk such that the bottom of the strainer bowl fits into it snuggly and without slop, and the annular underside of the workpiece just contacts the surface of the backing disk. I'll next mount the workpiece onto the backing disk by screwing into the waste pine cheeks, not the mahogany, with the two screws shown. These two screws hold near the rim of the workpiece which will allow me to finish-turn the upper surface of the wings adjacent to the bowl without hitting the screws.

    Because the workpiece will have to be dechucked and rechucked a couple of times to monitor the thickness of the bottom of the bowl and of the wings, pencil reference marks on the workpiece and on the backing disk so that you can be certain of rechucking the workpiece in the same orientation.

Figure 12.11   Finish-turning the inside wall and floor of the bowl. I'm turning inboard, and it was therefore easier to turn the hollow with the lathe running in reverse. Because the wall's surface is slightly concave, I used the detail gouge sharpened with a convex bevel shown in figure 12.12. This convex bevel shape greatly lessens the probabilty of crushing the bowl wall's inside surface with the gouge's heel.

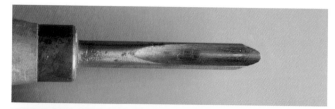

Figure 12.12   A 12-mm-wide detail gouge with a convex bevel ground as shown in figures 12.13 and 12.14. A convex bevel is preferred for turning surfaces which are concave in the direction in which the nose is to be traversed.

Figure 12.13 Grinding a convex bevel on the concave periphery of an 80-grit aluminium oxide grinding wheel. By varying the inclination of the gouge blade, I can vary the convexity or amount of hollow grind of the bevel.

Figure 12.14 Dressing a concave periphery into an 200-mm-diameter ginding wheel with a dressing stick. The radius of the concavity is here 17 mm. This is the smallest radius of curvature of surface which can be turned with the gouge blade presented horizontally.

Figure 12.15 Shear-scraping from the bottom of the wall "round the bend" into and across the floor of the bowl. By using the scraper with the top bevel shown in the figure 12.16, I'm able to present the edge with high side rake (highly skewed) and a small negative rake. I took the idea of using a scraper with a top bevel from an article by Melbourne turner Tracey Malady[6] and after an email conversation with American turner Tom Wirsing.

Figure 12.16   The scraper being used in figure 12.15. It's ground from the shank of a worn-down 9.5-mm-diameter HSS detail gouge. This tool has a top bevel which enables the wood to believe that the edge is being dragged while the tool is being pushed. *Negative-rake* is a term of tool presentation and not of tool geometry. Therefore this tool isn't a negative-rake scraper (all scrapers should be used with negative-rake-angle presentations), but one with a top or upper bevel.

Figure 12.18   Cutting away the outer waste, here with a 19-mm-wide detail gouge presented with high side rake. The workpiece is no longer held to the chucking plate by the two screws shown in figure 12.10. Instead it's chucked by being forced against the backing disk by a live tail center pressing onto a shallow plywood disk which fits snuggly against and into the rim of the strainer bowl. The friction generated between the underside of the wings and the right-hand face of the backing disk enables the turning to be accomplished.

Figure 12.17   Turning the outside of the bowl wall with a small-nosed detail gouge. The toolrest is aligned parallel to the bedways.

Figure 12.19 The top surface of the wings finish-turned. For this the workpiece can be just chucked by tailstock force as explained in figure 12.18.

Another chucking method which provides greater security and prevents any vibration or flexing of the wings uses the two screws whose heads are visible. Once the wings' thickness has been turned to within a few of millimeters of the finished thickness, the two screws shown were installed through the waste pine. Their heads are well recessed so that they won't be contacted during the turning or the sanding.

Figure 12.20 Marking the outsides of the wings. The plastic template is cut from a milk container. I used the calliper shown to monitor the wing thickness during the turning. To monitor the thickness between the floor and the bottom of the bowl I could have used the same calliper or a 1-mm-diameter twist drill which I poked through a strainer hole.

Figure 12.21 Sanding a concave wing edge with a drill-mounted sanding drum and abrasive sleeve.

13.4 ENDNOTES

1. Darlow, Mike. *Woodturning Design*. Exeter, NSW: The Melaleuca Press, 2003, p. 214.

2. Evan-Thomas, Owen. *Domestic Utensils of Wood*. London: Owen Evan-Thomas, 1932, plate 61.

3. Levi, Jonathan. *Treen for the Table*. Woodbridge, Suffolk: Antique Collectors' Club, 1998, page 179 shows three strainers.

4. Toller, Jane. *Treen and Other Turned Woodware for Collectors*. Newton Abbot: David & Charles, plate 1 shows a strainer which may not have been made specifically for negus.

5. Bradford, Sarah. *The Englishman's Wine, The Story of Port*. London: Christie's Wine Publications, 1983.

6. Malady, Tracey. "Negative Rake Scraper". *The Australian Woodworker*, Issue 203 February 2019, p. 31.

Chapter 13

AN IMPROVED PEPPER GRINDER

Pepper has long been the most important spice, and is still commonly dispensed from turned wooden pepper grinders. This is because once ground, dried pepper berries quickly lose their potency.

Many articles and at least one book[1] have been published on making pepper grinders. This chapter, however, introduces the spice before discussing grinder design and how to make the design of grinder shown in figure 13.1.

I prefer the term *pepper grinder* for hand-operated examples. *Pepper mill* implies that the grinding is powered by a means other than manpower. Battery powered versions such as that shown in figure 13.2 should therefore be called *mills*.

Figure 13.2 A pair of battery-operated pepper mills bought from the supermarket Aldi. The pair, batteries included, cost less than one of the Crushgrind mechanism used in the grinders shown in figure 13.1.

Figure 13.1 *Left to right*; pepper grinders turned from silky oak (*Grevillea robusta*), brush box (*Tristania conferta*), silky oak, and Manchurian pear (*Pyrus ussuriensis*).

13.1 PEPPER

Spices are derived from plant parts including bark, roots, flower buds, stigma, gums, resins, fruits or, in the case of pepper, its berries. Herbs come from the aromatic, herbaceous, leafy, green parts of plants.

Pepper is prepared from the berries of *Piper nigrum* (figure 13.3), a tropical perennial climbing vine of the *Piperaceae* family, probably originally native to the Malabar region along the southwest coast of India. Pepper is now grown in many tropical countries in large plantations on artificial towers about five meters high (figure 13.4). Vietnam is currently the major pepper producer; in 2013 it produced 163,000 tonnes of the total world pepper production of 473,000 tonnes.

The pepper berries turn from green to red as they ripen. Three processes are typically applied to the berries:

1. If the berries are picked before maturity and dried in the sun, they wrinkle and turn dark brown to produce black pepper.

2. If the berries are picked once mature, soaked, their outer skins rubbed away, and the pale seeds then dried, the product is white pepper.

3. Fresh pepper berries are also soaked in brine, vinegar, or in their own juice, and sold in jars or cans.

Green peppercorns are merely unripe pepper berries. Pink peppercorns come from the tree *Schinus molle* which is native to the Peruvian Andes, drought resistant, and therefore widely grown in arid regions.

Pepper spray isn't prepared from pepper, and is more accurately called *capsicum spray* because its active ingredient is the chemical compound capsaicin. This is derived from the fruits of some species of the *Capsicum* genus (which includes chillies), and is a lachrymatory agent which causes tears, eye pain, and temporary blindness.

Pepper trading before the sixteenth century

In Asia pepper has been used as a food flavoring from at least 2000 BC. Black peppercorns were found stuffed in the nostrils of Ramesses II who was mummified in Egypt in 1213 BC. Pepper has been used in Europe from Roman times.

Prior to the European takeover of the spice trade in the 16th century, pepper destined for Europe, the Middle East and Africa was bought in southwest India by Arab traders, and then shipped westwards across the Arabian Sea. The then main Indian export port for pepper is called Kozhikode by Indians, but was also known by its Arab name Qaliqut or Calicut (figure 13.5).

The ease of sailing to and fro across the Arabian Sea (the northern part of the Indian Ocean to the west of India) depends on the time of year. The trade winds blow from southwest to northeast throughout the year. However in the northern-hemisphere spring and summer the Indian subcontinent heats faster than the sea, creating the northeast monsoon winds favorable to sailing from Africa and Arabia to India. In the autumn and winter the reverse occurs. The winds associated with the

Figure 13.3   The vine *Piper nigrum*.
Photograph by Axel Steenberg, sourced from Wikimedia Commons.

Figure 13.4   Pepper vines growing in Kampot, Vietnam.
Sourced from Wikimedia Commons.

Figure 13.5   View of Calicut from Georg Braun's and Franz Hogenber's 1572 atlas *Civitates orbis terrarium*.
Sourced from Wikimedia Commons.

resulting southwest monsoon are stronger than the trade winds, and allow spice-laden ships to sail west. The pepper-carrying ships therefore usually sailed from India in October. After crossing the Arabian Sea, pepper bound for Europe was shipped up the Red Sea rather than the Persian Gulf, carried by camel train to Alexandria and other ports on the eastern Mediterranean coast, and thence by ship to European ports including Venice and Genoa.

The freight costs and the number of middle men involved in transporting pepper and other Asian spices such as nutmeg, cloves, and cinnamon ensured that spices were hugely expensive in Europe. The potential profits from the spice trade were a major incentive for European kingdoms on the Atlantic coast to take that trade over. In the van was Portugal.

Portugal became a separate kingdom during the twelfth century; it commenced its efforts to acquire a trading empire in 1415 when it invaded the Barbary pirate base of Ceuta, opposite Gibraltar, in what is now Morocco.

The third son of Portugal's king John 1, known subsequently as Henry the Navigator (figure 13.6), took part in the invasion of Ceuta. Its success spurred Henry's promotion of exploration in the Atlantic Ocean and down the west coast of Africa. Henry also promoted the development of a new type of sailing ship better suited for exploration, the caravel (figure 13.7).

Henry died in 1460, but Portuguese exploration continued. In 1486 king John II of Portugal appointed Bartolomeu Dias to lead an expedition to discover a trade route to India. In early 1488 Dias passed what he called the Cape of Storms—John II later renamed that cape the Cape of Good Hope. Dias's mission was however frustrated shortly after rounding the southern tip of Africa when his crew demanded to return to Portugal.

Through the 1494 treaty of Tordesillas, signed in the north-central Spanish town of that name, Spain and Portugal agreed to divide newly discovered lands between themselves. With some exceptions Spain had exclusive rights to lands to the west of a line of longitude running through the center of the north Atlantic, and Portugal had exclusive rights to lands to the east of that line. The treaty didn't attempt to clarify where their respective exclusive zones met on the opposite side of the Earth. (Europeans didn't know in 1494 that there was a Pacific Ocean. It was first sighted in 1513, and not reached by Ferdinand Magellan until 1521. He named

Figure 13.6 Prince Henry the Navigator (1394–1460).

Sourced from Wikimedia Commons.

BARTHOLOMEW DIAZ ON HIS VOYAGE TO THE CAPE.

Figure 13.7 The caravels *Sao Cristovao* and *Sao Pantaleao* commanded by Bartolomeu Dias. Caravels were developed from Portuguese fishing boats in the middle of the 15th century under the sponsorship of Henry the Navigator. They were lateen-rigged and had a shallow keel. Scanned from page 314 of the 1887 book *The Sea: Its Stirring Story of Adventure, Peril and Heroism*, Volume 2.

Sourced from Wikimedia Commons.

it the Mar Pacifico). Although the treaty of Tordesillas was confirmed by pope Alexander VI, it was ignored by other maritime powers.

In 1496 king John II selected Vasco da Gama (figure 14.8) to lead a four-ship expedition to complete Dias's task. Da Gama left Lisbon in July 1497, and reached Calicut on 20 May 1498. Laden with spices, Da Gama left Calicut on 29 August 1498 and reached Lisbon a year later. The spices acquired ensured that the expedition was immensely profitable, and spurred further spice-related trade and conquest by Portugal, and later other by European kingdoms with Atlantic coastlines.

Figure 13.8 Vasco da Gama (c1469–1524). Portrait painted in 1838, now in National Maritime Museum, Greenwich Hospital.
Sourced from Wikimedia Commons.

Figure 13.9 A crinoline, a type of structural petticoat constructed of spring steel hoops or a wire helix suspended and spaced using fabric strips.
Sourced from Wikimedia Commons.

13.2 DEVELOPMENT OF THE PEPPER GRINDER

The pepper grinder, which displaced the pestle and mortar for grinding pepper, was a French invention. In 1810 the brothers Jean-Frédéric and Jean-Pierre II Peugeot began making steel and forging it into blades and springs at Valentigney, near to the Swiss border. In 1842 the firm split. The three sons of Jean-Pierre II together with nephew Armand Peugeot concentrated on making spring-steel crinoline cages (figure 13.9), and during the 1850s were producing up to 25,000 per month. In the 1860s their business Peugeot Frères started making kitchen-related products, but didn't begin to manufacture pepper grinders until 1874. The pepper-grinding mechanism was derived from that used in the coffee grinders which they were already manufacturing. Peugeot still manufactures pepper grinders, but their grinding mechanism is no longer available separately. Because its patent is long expired, similar mechanisms and grinders are available from other manufacturers.

Peugeot Frères didn't stop at pepper grinders. In 1887 it started to manufacture safety bicycles, in 1889 it launched a steam-powered tricycle, and in 1892 started to manufacturing motor cars. In 1896 nephew Armand broke away and concentrated on manufacturing motor cars. Armand having no heir, the two Peugeot companies merged back together in 1910.

The CrushGrind mechanism (figure 13.10) used in this chapter's grinder design was invented by Ken Muff Lassen, a Dane. Launched in 1994, it offers a distinct alternative to the Peugeot mechanism (which it resembles), and is readily available for installation by woodturners.

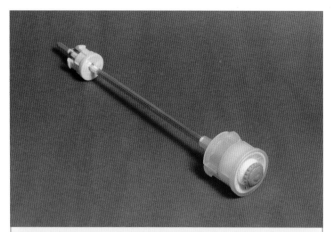

Figure 13.10 The Danish CrushGrind mechanism works in much the same way as the Peugeot type, but the CrushGrind's grinding parts are ceramic. The CrushGrind has three components: a grinding drum, an aluminium pentagonal (five-sided) shaft with a chamfered top, and a collar which can slide along the shaft and is fixed into a grinder's cap. The mechanism is bulkier than the Peugeot-type, but seems to give better control over how finely the pepper is ground.

CrushGrind mechanisms with shafts are available in two nominal lengths: 260 mm and 470 mm. This article's grinder uses the shorter mechanism.

Care needs to be taken when installing a CrushGrind mechanism into a grinder's wooden cap and body because of the tight fits. I've opted to glue the drum and collar in with epoxy rather than use dry fitting which demands precise enlargements of the bored holes.

13.3 PEPPER-GRINDER DESIGN

A pepper grinder should:

1. be easy to fill
2. have sufficient pepper capacity
3. have a body and cap which can be readily and separately gripped
4. not be easily knocked over.

Most pepper grinders have two wooden parts, a body and a cap. These parts are bored with holes of several

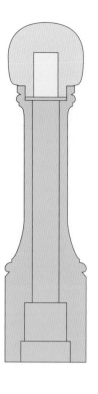

Figure 13.11 A cross-section through the two wooden parts of a typical commercial pepper grinder.

diameters, and are turned in low relief (figure 13.11). Larger-capacity, commercially-made pepper grinders are usually excessively tall relative to their base diameters which ensures that they fail to satisfy requirements 1 and 4 above. Figure 13.12 shows a design which better satisfies the above four requirements.

14.4 MAKING THE GRINDER

The making process is described in figures 13.13 to 13.31, and in summary is:

1. Turn the starting blank as shown in figures 13.13 and 13.4, and saw it through the two small-diameter sections into a base, a middle, and a cap workpiece
2. If you don't have to complete the grinder immediately, bore the three workpieces while holding them by their chucking spigots with drills which will produce undersize holes. Then leave the workpieces for a couple of weeks to fully season
3. Chuck the seasoned base workpiece by its bottom spigot, and flatten its right-hand end. In doing so

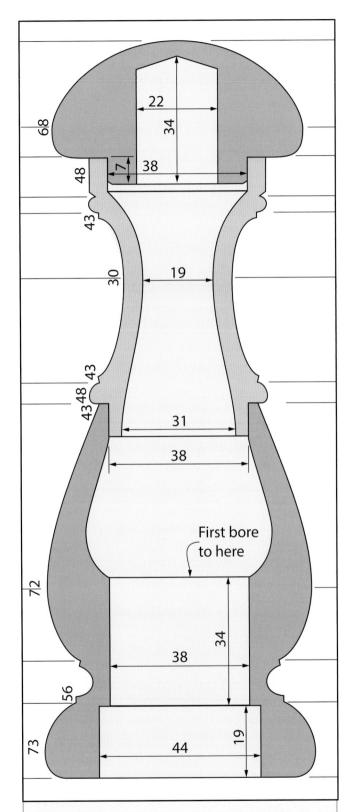

Figure 13.12 My design of pepper grinder has three wooden parts: a base and a middle section (which when glued together form the body), and a cap.

take care not to trim too much off or the bottom workpiece cannot be rechucked by its right-hand chucking spigot. Bore a 38-mm-diameter hole to the depth indicated in figure 13.12 as shown in figure 13.15.

4. If you choose, perform the optional hollowing labelled in figure 13.13 as shown in figure 13.16.

5. Dechuck the base workpiece and rechuck it by its top spigot, flatten its right-hand end, finish boring the 38 mm diameter hole, and widen that hole's right-hand end to a depth of 19 mm and to at least 44-mm diameter (figure 13.17). Sand the surfaces which will be visible on the finished grinder.

6. Chuck the middle workpiece by its bottom spigot, flatten its right-hand (top) end, bore the 19 mm hole right through (figure 13.18), bore the 38 mm diameter hole to a depth of 9 mm hole (figure 13.19), and flare the right-hand end of the 19-mm-diameter hole (figure 13.20). As before, when flattening the end of the right-hand spigot, the spigot must be left long-enough to be used to rechuck the workpiece for the next operation. Sand the cylindrical surface of the 38-mm-diameter hole.

7. Dechuck the middle workpiece, chuck it by its top spigot, flatten its right-hand spigot's end, if necessary finish boring the 19-mm-diameter hole, and finish-turn the spigot which will be glued into the 38 mm diameter hole in the top of the base and the adjacent shoulder (figure 13.21). Also flare the through hole to 31-mm diameter using the method shown in figure 13.20.

8. With the middle workpiece still chucked by its top spigot, glue the base and middle workpieces together (figure 13.22).

9. Mount the body between two plugs (figure 13.23) and finish-turn and sand it (figure 13.24).

10. Chuck the cap workpiece by its top spigot, finish-turn its right-hand (bottom) end, checking that the spigot is a nice (neither tight nor loose) fit into the 38 mm hole in the top of the body, bore the 22 mm diameter hole (figure 13.25), and sand the finish-turned surfaces.

11. Chuck the cap workpiece on a wooden pin chuck (figure 13.26). Finish-turn the remainder of the cap

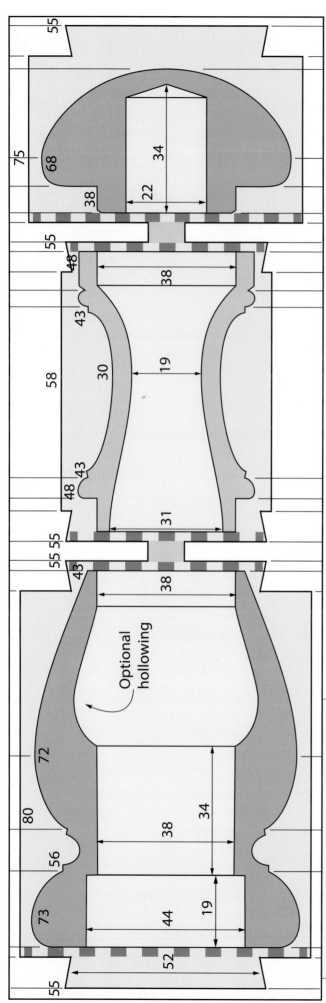

Optional hollowing

(figure 13.27). To ensure that the cap's surface has a consistent appearance, perform the sanding with the lathe running in reverse.

12. It's better to polish the body and the cap before gluing in the CrushGrind mechanism's drum and collar because this allows the lathe to be used for the polishing operations. I use a water-based polyurethane for pale woods so as not to tint them.

13. The CrushGrind's shaft as supplied is too long for this design of pepper grinder. Because that shaft is aluminium, if you shorten it by hacksawing and then grind the chamfer around its top after its attached drum has been glued into the body, the shaft is likely to get bent. The grinder won't then work nicely. It's therefore preferable to shorten the shaft as calculated in figure 13.28 and chamfer its free (top) end before gluing the drum into the body.

14. Use the hacksawn-off section of shaft to make the simple tool shown on the right-hand side of figure 13.29.

15. Saw the plastic lugs shown in figure 13.30 off the CrushGrind grinding drum.

16. Prepare the two plugs shown in figure 13.31

17. Mix a suitable quantity of epoxy resin (don't use a quick-setting type)

18. Apply resin fairly sparingly to the inside of the 38 mm diameter hole in the bottom of the body and to the outside of the drum. Press the drum into the body as indicated in figure 13.31.

Figure 13.13 The pencil gauge for my design of pepper grinder for the single blank which is subsequently sawn through the two narrow sections into a base, a middle and a cap workpiece.

The subsequent turning processes assume that you have a scroll chuck with jaws which are designed to grip chucking spigots with a minimum diameter of 52 mm (2 inches).

Make two copies of this gauge and glue them onto card or thin plywood. Cut one into three separate pencil gauges.

The blue-dashed liness represent wood which is cut away using the long point of a skew to leave flat, finished surfaces.

19. After applying epoxy similarly, hold the cap in one hand and using the tool shown in figure 13.29, force the sliding collar into the hole in the cap.

Although the above sequence and the need for wooden plugs are somewhat complicated, the resulting grinder is well worth the effort as figure 13.1 confirms.

Figure 13.16 Removing the optional waste labelled in figure 13.13 with a 10-mm spindle-detail gouge. Alternatively you could use a narrow, round-nosed scraper.

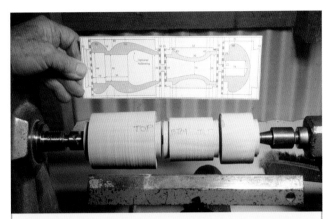

Figure 13.14 The starting blank turned to the configuration shown on the figure 13.13 pencil gauge held above. I cut the two narrow sections to about 10-mm-diameter with a 2-mm-wide parting tool.

Figure 13.17 The base workpiece has been dechucked, transposed and rechucked by its slightly-shortened top spigot. The now right-hand end of the base workpiece has been flattened with the long point of a skew, the remainder of the 38-mm-diameter hole has been bored, and the right-hand end of that hole widened out to 44-mm diameter with a square-ended scraper.

Figure 13.15 The base workpiece is first chucked by its bottom spigot. The right-hand end has been flattened with the long point of a skew. The resulting surface must truly flat or a gap may be visible at the later-glued junction between the base and middle parts. A 38-mm (or 1 1/2 inch = 38.1 mm) diameter hole is then bored to the level shown in figure 13.12.

Figure 13.18 The middle workpiece is first chucked by its bottom spigot. The right-hand chucking spigot has been slightly shortened to a flat surface using a skew's long point. Here the middle workpiece is being bored with a 19 mm diameter twist drill. The white tape depth marker is to remind me not to bore too far and thus prevent the drill hitting the chuck jaws.

Figure 13.20 With the middle part still chucked by its bottom spigot, flaring the hole between where the hole is left at 19 mm diameter and the 38 mm diameter hole section. I'm using a 10 mm spindle-detail gouge.

Figure 13.19 The middle workpiece is still chucked by its bottom spigot. The shallow 38-mm-diameter hole is then bored into the top end of the middle part with a 38-mm-diameter drill.

Figure 13.21 With the middle part now chucked by its shortened top spigot, bore the remainder of the 19-mm-diameter hole, cut to a nice fit the spigot which will be glued into the 38-mm-diameter hole in the top of the bottom workpiece, and flare the right-hand end of the through hole as shown in figure 13.20.

Figure 13.22 Gluing the base and middle workpieces together, here with cross-linked PVA glue. Take care to align the grain in the two workpieces. A plug with a 44-mm-diameter spigot is housed in the right-hand end of the base, and allows the tailstock to force and hold the two parts together until the glue has set.

Figure 13.24 The body finish-turned. It will be polished when the cap has been bored and finish-turned about to be polished.

Figure 13.25 With the cap workpiece chucked by its top spigot, the bottom part of the cap has been finish-turned, and the 22-mm-diameter, 34-mm-deep hole has been bored.

Figure 13.23 Mounting the two-part body workpiece between a plug with a 38-mm-diameter pin held in the scroll chuck and the plug shown in figure 13.22 which locates in the body's right-hand (bottom) end and is axially located by a live tail center.

Figure 13.26   Mounting the cap on a 22-mm-diameter wooden pin chuck to complete the finish-turning and sanding of the cap.

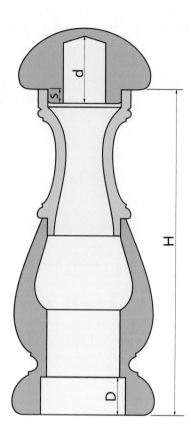

Figure 13.27   Finish-turning the remainder of the cap. I'm using a 19-mm detail gouge whose blade cross section has the correct semicircle of steel below the bottom of the flute. Alas this gouge size is no longer manufactured.

The Crushgrind mechanism's collar is later epoxied into the bored hole in the cap (see figure 13.29).

Figure 13.28   Determining the shortening of the CrushGrind shaft. This shortening is calculated using the formula:

$$\text{Shortening} = L - \{(H - D) + (d - s)\}$$

where L is the length from the top of the CrushGrind shaft down to the top of the rim at the bottom of the 38 mm diameter part of the mechanism. L equals 250 mm for a new mechanism.

If you turned and bored the grinder exactly to the dimensions shown in figure 14.12, you'd have to shorten the mechanism's stem by

$$250 - \{(164 - 19) + (34 - 7)\} = 78 \text{ mm}$$

If you shorten the shaft too much, the sliding collar, which is glued into the cap, won't grip the shaft properly, and therefore you won't be able to lift the grinder by its cap alone. To prevent **>**

> this, don't bore the cap to less than 34 mm, and accurately measure the length by which the shaft has to be shortened.

After shortening the shaft, chamfer its free end on a bench grinder or similar, or with a file.

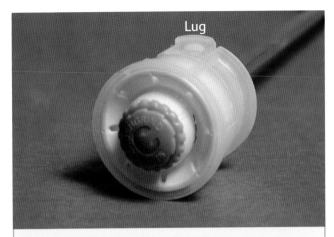

Figure 13.30 The CrushGrind's grinding drum. Both of its projecting lugs are best sawn off before epoxying it into the grinder's body.

Figure 13.29 Gluing the sliding collar into the cap.

To make the tool on the right, the length of shaft hacksawn off earlier has been hammered into a 6-mm-diameter hole bored into a wooden handle so that no more than 34 mm projects.

To glue the collar into the cap the collar is first pushed onto the tool's shaft. Epoxy is then smeered onto the outside of the larger diameter part of the collar and onto the inside of the hole in the cap. The collar is then forced into the hole using the tool.

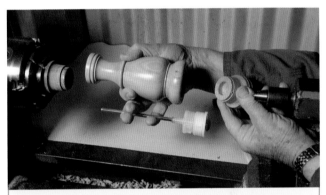

Figure 13.31 Epoxying the grinding drum with the shortened shaft into the grinder's body. To enable in-lathe cramping, a 7-mm-diameter hole has been bored through the plug here held in the scroll chuck and shown earlier in figure 13.23. An additional wooden plug with shallow recess in its left-hand end to house the serated knob at the right-hand end of the drum end allows the tailstock to be used to force the drum into its hole.

13.5 ENDNOTES

1. West, Chris. *Turning Salt and Pepper Shakers and Mills*. Lewes: Guild of Master Craftsman Publications, 2011.

A POINT-PRESSER-AND-CLAPPER

The point-presser-and-clappper was unknown to me until my wife asked me to replicate the commercial example shown in figure 14.1. This strangely named tool is used by dressmakers and tailors to press seams flat. The bottom part, the clapper, is used for general pressing. The top part, the point-presser, is used with an iron to press the seams at sharp corners such as the points of collars or lapels.

14.1 DESIGN

Commercial versions typically are made of two parts, with the top part cut from a plank about 19 mm thick and having its grain horizontal. Dowels, biscuits or long screws are used to fix the two parts together. The design featured in this chapter is shown in figure 14.2. As you would expect, it includes turnings, and is both stronger and more attractive than most of the commercial examples.

Figures 14.3, 14.4 and 14.5 show the dimensions for my point-presser-and-clapper. The two stub columns in

figure 14.5 can be turned from the same wood as the other two parts or from a wood with a contrasting color.

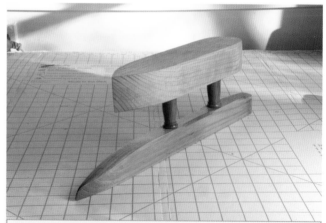

Figure 14.2 The point-presser-and-clapper described in this chapter. *Top*, the right way up: *bottom*, showing how the point-presser is shaped.
The clapper and point-presser are in mountain ash (*Eucalyptus regnans*), the columns are in Honduras mahaogany (*Swietenia macrophylla*).

Figure 14.1 A commercially-manufactured point-presser-and-clapper made from radiata pine (*Pinus radiata*). Some brands have the area of the top part within the dashed line cut away.

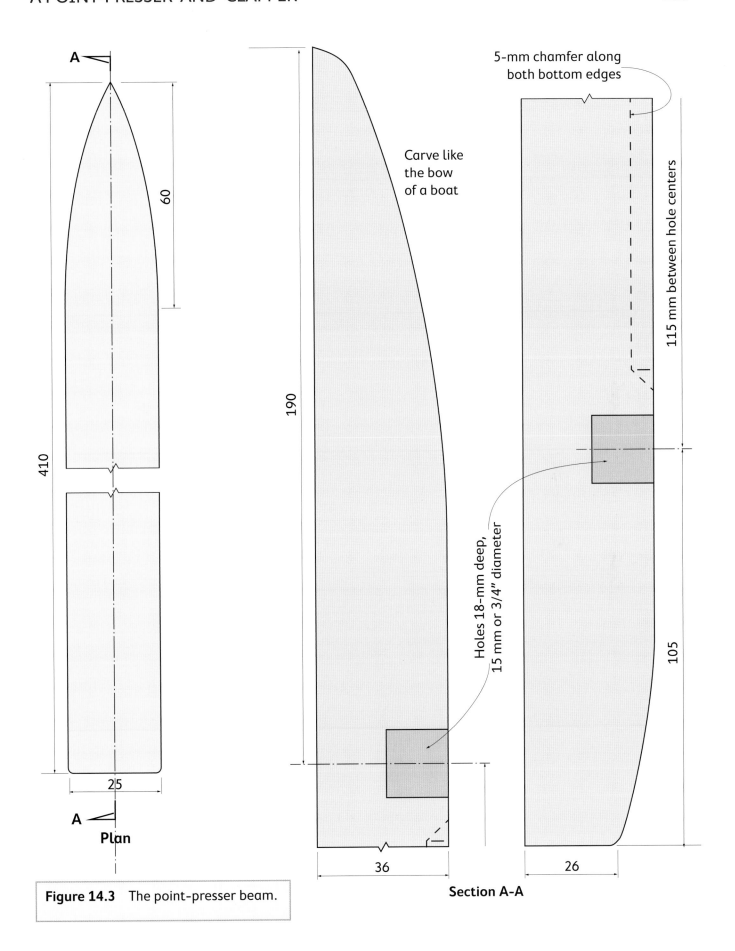

Figure 14.3 The point-presser beam.

Section A-A

Plan

Carve like
the bow
of a boat

5-mm chamfer along
both bottom edges

Holes 18-mm deep,
15 mm or 3/4" diameter

115 mm between hole centers

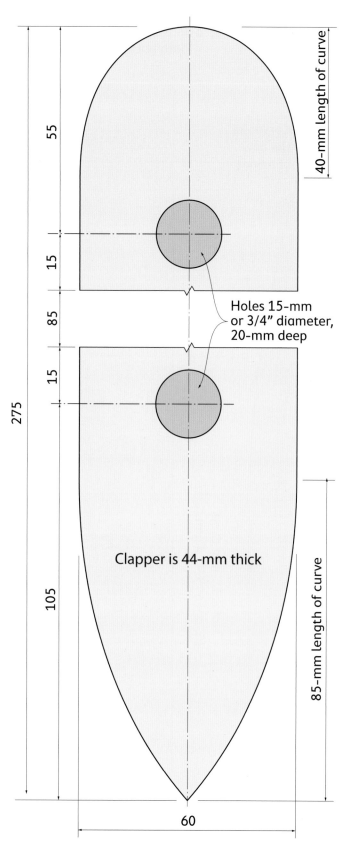

Holes 15-mm or 3/4" diameter, 20-mm deep

Clapper is 44-mm thick

Figure 14.4   The clapper in plan.

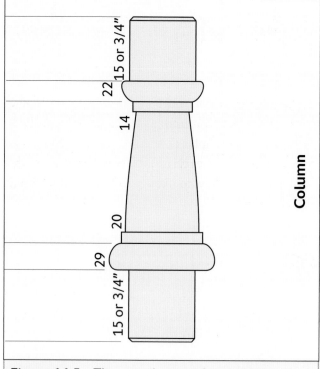

Figure 14.5   The pencil gauge for the stub columns.

14.2   MAKING

I used a 3/4-inch drill to produce the holes into which the pins on the columns are glued. If you can only access drills sized in millimeters, I suggest 15-mm diameter.

Chapter 15

REEL STANDS

The terms *spool*, *bobbin* and *reel* seem to be interchangeable, although *reel* continues to be associated with sewing thread. This chapter describes the events which led to the invention of the reel stand. The second part of this chapter describes how to make a reel stand which holds 48 standard reels.

15.1   ANTIQUE REEL STANDS

Reel stands are attractive objects as the antique examples shown in figures 15.1 to 15.5 confirm. They're also functional; for example, thread from a reel on a reel stand can be used to directly thread a sewing machine. Reel stands started to be made in the 1820s. Early examples were wood, and wood reel stands continue to be made. Metal, usually brass, stands started to be manufactured in about 1870.

Figure 15.2   Mahogany reel stand, 25.5-cm high x 13.5-cm maximum diameter. Three of the wood and ivory pins are missing. The top cup is intended to hold a pin cushion.
    Illustration courtesy of Prichard Antiques, Winchcombe, UK.

Figure 15.1   Mahogany reel stand with pin cushion. Height to top of pin cushion 20 cm, maximum diameter 12.8 cm.

Figure 15.3   American-made mahogany reel stand with drawer and pin cushion.

Illustration scanned from: Whiting, Gertrude. *Tools & Toys of Stitchery.* New York: Dover Publications, p. 23. (Originally published in 1928 by Columbia University Press.)

Figure 15.5   Brass reel stands. Two similar brass reel stands are pictured in: Taunton, Nerylla. *Antique Needlework Tools and Embroideries.* Woodbridge: Antique Collectors' Club, 2006, p. 166. Metal reel stands started to be manufactured in about 1870.

Illustration courtesy of London Auctions, Chiswick, UK.

Figure 15.4   Magogany and Brazilian rosewood reel stand, 17 cm x 10 cm.

Illustration courtesy of Woody's Antiques, Northamptonshire, UK.

15.2 HISTORY

Sewing thread started to be sold wound on reels in about 1820, and this triggered the invention of the reel stand. Until then thread was supplied in hanks, also called skeins. The timing of this change in how sewing thread was sold resulted from Britain's Industrial Revolution and the Napoleonic Wars.

15.2.1 Advances in the manufacture of cotton cloth

Inventions and developments in England during the eighteenth and early nineteenth century transformed the production of cotton cloth from an insignificant cottage industry unable to compete with imported Indian calicoes and muslins into one of the two drivers of Britain's Industrial Revolution. (The other driver was the iron industry.)

The first transformative invention was the flying shuttle which John Kay (1704–1779) patented in 1733. (His memorial is shown in figure 15.6.) Kay's shuttle was wheeled and ran on a race or track in a hand-operated loom. When the weaver jerked a cord, a paddle kicked the shuttle which held weft yarn across the warp yarns which run lengthways in a loom. Widely adopted from 1760 after his son Robert's invention of the drop box, the Kays' inventions greatly increased the productivity of hand weaving-looms.

Carding immediately preceeds spinning. In carding, unorganised clumps of fibres are cleaned of extraneous matter and disentangled. The separated fibres are then aligned parallel with each other. Hand carding uses two wire brushes called *cards*. Lewis Paul's rotary carding machine, patented in 1748, speeded the processing prior to spinning.

Even before the introduction of Kay's flying shuttle, it took four spinners to service a loom. Cloth production was therefore restricted by the shortage of spinners. And because spinners were usually women, the bottleneck was particularly serious at harvest time. Hence the importance of James Hargreaves' spinning jenny invented in about 1764 (figure 15.7). The word *jenny*, like *gin* which will be mentioned shortly, is a contraction

Figure 15.6 The John Kay Memorial erected in 1908 in his birthplace, Bury, Lancashire, The memorial was paid for by Kay's great-great grandson. There isn't extant portrait which is undisputably of John Kay.
Sourced from Wikimedia Commons.

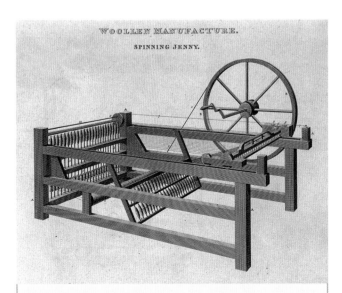

Figure 15.7 A spinning jenny engraved in 1811.
Sourced from Wellcome Images.

Figure 15.8 Richard Arkwright (1732–1792) who Kenneth Clark on page 236 of his book *Civilisation* opined was "typical of the new potentates who were to dominate industry until the present day". This portrait, now in the Derby Museum & Art Gallery, was painted in 1790 by Joseph Wright of Derby,.
Sourced from Wikimedia Commons.

Figure 15.9 Samuel Crompton (1753–1827). Sourced from Wikimedia Commons.

of *engine* which also then meant machine. Hargreaves' jenny had multiple (initially eight) spindles and greatly speeded yarn spinning, although the yarns produced were only suitable for the weft. The weft is produced by passing the yarn-carrying shuttle back and forth across the warp. (Warp yarns for cotton cloth were typically linen at that time.)

Richard Arkwright (figure 15.8) advanced advanced the manufacture of cotton cloth in three ways:

1. He invented a better yarn-spinning machine than the jenny, which, patented in 1769, spun a cotton yarn strong enough to be used for both warp and weft.

Initially driven by horses, the machine later came to be called a *water-frame* because in 1771 Arkwright and others commenced building a water-powered spinning mill at Cromford in Derbyshire.

2. In 1775 Arkwright patented a carding machine which enabled the supply of carded fibre to keep up with the spinning machines

3. Arkwright's third advance was to establish machine-based factory production using relatively unskilled labor as the ideal method to produce efficiently and in volume. (The first true British factory was a silk throwing mill built for Thomas Lombe which opened in 1719 in Derby.)

Samuel Crompton (figure 15.9) had around 1770 begun to spin cotton yarn for the family hand loom using an early version of Hargreaves' spinning jenny. The spinning machine he developed in about 1778 was later dubbed a *mule* because it combined features of Hargreaves' jenny and Arkwright's water frame. It produced a smoother and finer yarn.

An American invention also facilitated an expansion in cotton yarn production. The cotton bolls had to be cleaned by hand before being exported, a labor-intensive process until Eli Whitney invented the cotton gin which he patented in 1793 (figure 15.10).

The above and other inventions and developments transformed Britain's cloth production from one based on wool augmented by silk and linen to one dominated by cotton. This change arose because cotton was better suited to mechanised production and raw cotton production was able to expand rapidly (by 800% between 1780 and 1800) to satisfy the increasing demand. Cotton cloth thus rapidly became cheaper than the alternatives, and was also more washable and more wearable. The explosion in the production of cotton cloth in turn increased the demand for sewing thread.

Figure 15.10 Eli Whitney's cotton gin. The cotton bols are fed in from the left, and dragged through a comb by the roller with projecting wires, thus separating the seeds.
Sourced from Wikimedia Commons.

15.2.2 History of cotton sewing thread

Sewing thread needs to be strong, flexible, and somewhat slippery. Throughout the 18th century sewing thread was made from natural silk or, for coarse sewing, linen. During the Napoleonic Wars which lasted from 1803 to 1815 trade between Britain and mainland Europe was curtailed, particularly after Napoleon issued the Berlin Decree on 20 November 1806. This decree introduced the Continental System which forbade trade between Britain and Europe. The importation of silk and silk thread into Britain was therefore strangled. In response Patrick Clark (who with his brother James ran a heddle-yarn-spinning business in Paisley on the western outskirts of Glasgow) developed a method of spinning cotton heddle-yarn to replace the silk heddle-yarn which the business had been producing. (A *heddle* is a 'loom part which is used to separate the warp threads'.) James and Patrick also developed a method to spin an excellent cotton sewing thread.

In 1812 two of the sons of James Clark (James (1783–1865) shown in figure 15.11 and John (1791–1864))

Figure 15.11 James Clark, inventor of the cotton reel.
Scanned from: Blair, Matthew. *The Paisley Thread Industry*. Paisley: Alexander Gardner, 1907, p. 43.

opened a new mill in which to produce the cotton sewing thread. It was this son, James, who invented the cotton reel. In about 1820 therefore the brothers' company J. & J. Clark started to sell its cotton sewing thread on wooden cotton reels instead of in hanks or skeins. These reels were produced by local woodturner Robert Paul (the turning shop shown in figure 15.12 is not Paul's). Figure 15.13 shows several 20th-century wooden reels turned on automatic lathes. Today reels are invariably moulded in plastic.

At first, customers were charged a half-penny for the reel, but this sum was refundable if a reel was returned. Alternatively a customer could have a reel reloaded with fresh thread. Initially the thread was wound onto reels by hand, but machine winding was soon introduced, and in 1846 John Clark invented an improved machine which continued to be used for decades.[2]

Demand for cotton sewing thread was further stimulated by the introduction and spread of power-looms

which both lowered the cost and increased the supply of cloth. Edmund Cartright invented one in 1787, but it wasn't until the 1820s that power-looms started to displace hand weaving.

A further impetus to the demand for cotton sewing thread was the invention and rapid take-up of the sew-

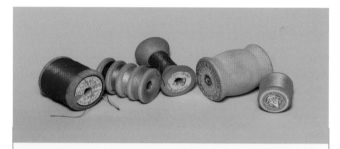

Figure 15.13   Wooden thread reels turned on automatic lathes. Thread reels are now usually moulded in plastic.

Figure 15.12   Turning cotton reels in Ferguslie, a suburb of Paisley, in 1887. Courtesy of Paisley Thread Mill Museum.

ing machine. From conception, by Englishman Charles Weisenthal in 1755, to the first practical realisation by American Elias Howe took ninety years. Then Isaac Merritt Singer (figure 15.14) became involved. While working in a machine shop in Boston, Massachusetts, in 1851 Singer was asked to repair a Howe sewing machine. Within eleven days he had produced a better version, and went on to dominate the supply of sewing machine well into the 20th century (figure 15.15).

Machine sewing required a more flexible thread than hand sewing. Again a member of the Clark family, George Aitken Clark (1823–1873), a grandson of Patrick, answered the need by introducing in 1864 what he called Our New Thread or O.N.T.

There is a connection, one might call it a *thread*, joining Arkwright to the Clarks. Kenneth Clark was Britain's most notable art historian and art administrator during the middle decades of the 20th century. On page 1 of his

entertaining autobiography *Another Part of the Wood*[2] Clark mentions that "my great, great grandfather [James Clark] invented the cotton spool". Kenneth Clark was also the author and presenter of the hugely popular, 13 episode, television series *Civilisation* first broadcast in February 1969. In the book of the series Clark refers to Wright of Derby, the painter of Arkwright's portrait shown in figure 15.8 as "a mediocrity".[3] As a painter maybe, but Wright's depictions of persons and events of the early Industrial Revolution remain highly valued.

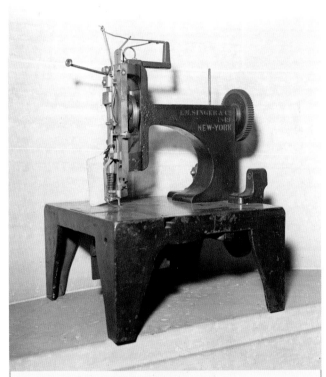

Figure 15.15 An early Singer sewing machine. Sourced from Wikimedia Commons.

Figure 15.14 Isaac Merritt Singer (1824 1887) painted in 1889 by Edward Harrison May. Sourced from Wikimedia Commons.

15.3   MAKING THE REEL STAND

Reel stands seem to have been a popular woodturning project as shown by figures 15.1 to 15.4. My reel stand design is shown in figures 15.16 to 15.23, but there's plenty of scope to design one yourself.

There are no special turning techniques involved, but below I list some points to bear in mind:

- The plates shown in figures 15.22 and 15.23 are ideally turned from quarter-sawn stock to minimise cupping.

- The eight knobs (figure 15.20), the four shallow feet (figure 15.18), and the column (figure 15.21) con-

taining the pin cushion (figure 15.9) are cupchuck turned.

- Drill the holes for the four shallow feet at the four corners of a square whose sides are parallel and at right angles to the bottom plate's wood grain so that the stand will be stable if the bottom plate cups.

- When drilling the holes for the brass rods and gluing the parts together, align the grain in the plates and the visible growth rings in the column, pincushion holder and feet.

- Polish the separate components in the lathe before assembly. I held the knobs by pushing them onto a wooden pin projecting from a cupchucked, axially-grained piece of waste wood.

- I indented the top end of each brass rod by squeezing it with pliers. I then glued the indented rod end into the hole in its wooden knob with epoxy. The indentations ensured that the rod was securely held in its knob.

Figure 15.16   The reel stand whose dimensions are shown in figure 15.7. This stand is turned from Honduras mahogany; it holds 48 standard cotton reels. The high, central cup is for a pin cushion.

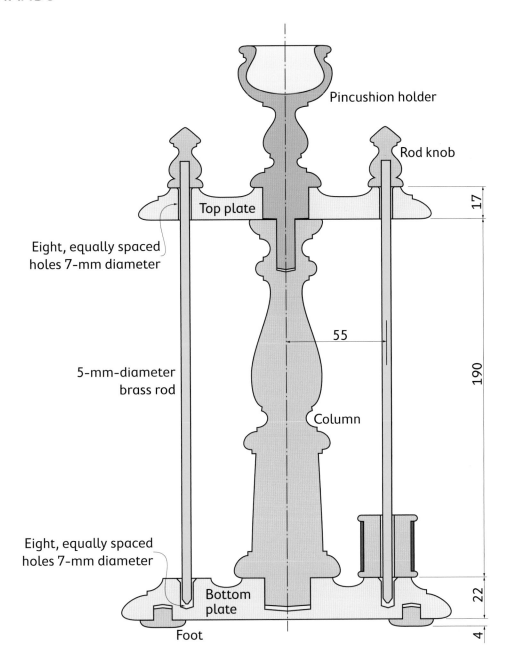

Pincushion holder

Rod knob

Top plate

Eight, equally spaced
holes 7-mm diameter

5-mm-diameter
brass rod

55

190

17

Column

Eight, equally spaced
holes 7-mm diameter

Bottom
plate

22

Foot

4

Figure 15.17   A half-size section through the reel stand pictured in figure 16.16.

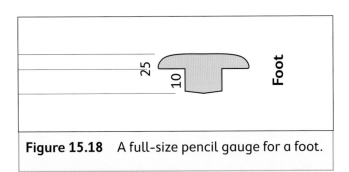

25

10

Foot

Figure 15.18   A full-size pencil gauge for a foot.

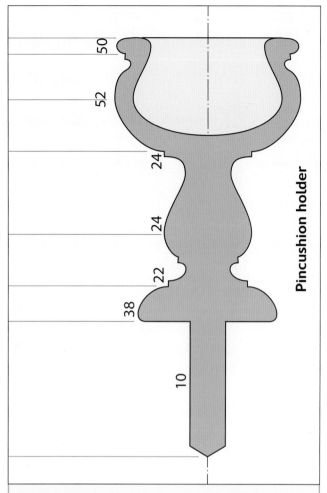

Figure 15.19 A full-size pencil gauge for the pincushion holder.

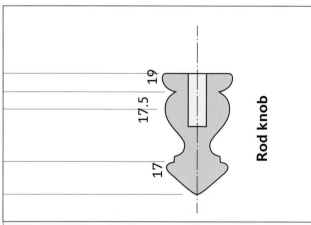

Figure 15.20 A full-size section pencil gauge for a rod knob.

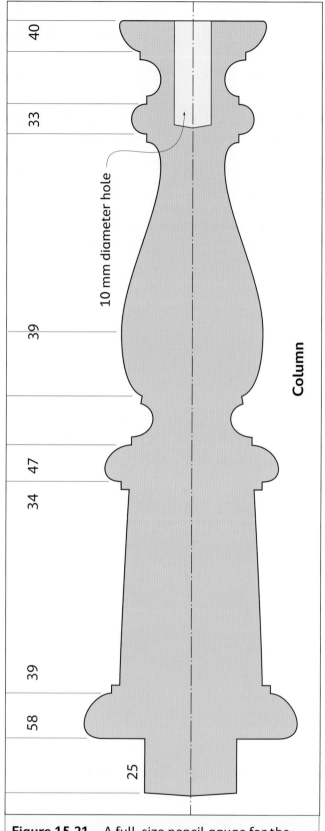

Figure 15.21 A full-size pencil gauge for the column.

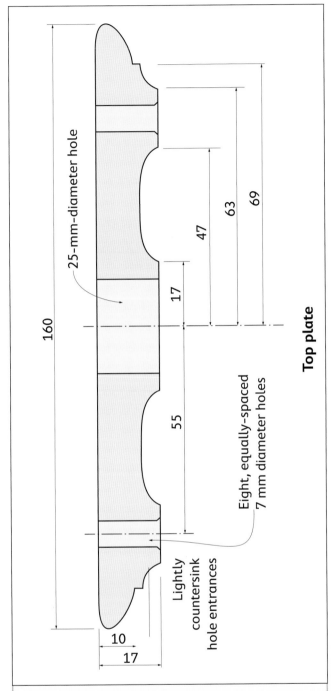

Figure 15.22 A full-size pencil gauge for the top plate.

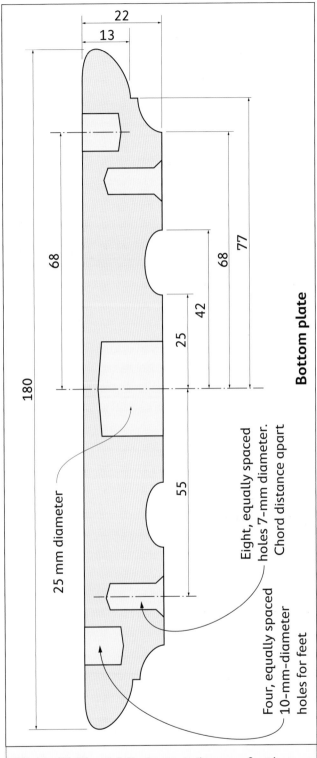

Figure 15.23 A full-size pencil gauge for the bottom plate.

15.4   ENDNOTES

1. Taunton, Nerylla. *Antique Needlework Tools*. Woodbridge: Antique Collectors' Club, 1997.

2. Blair, Matthew. *The Paisley Thread Industry*. Paisley: Alexander Gardner, 1907, p. 34–43.

3. Clark, Kenneth. *Another Part of the Wood: A Self Portrait*. London: HarperCollins, 1975. Also well worth reading is: Stourton, James. *Kenneth Clark: Life, Art and Civilisation*. London: William Collins, 2016.

4. Clark, Kenneth. *Civilisation*. London: BBC Books, 1969, p. 340.

Chapter 16

SPINNING TOPS

Figure 16.1 A selection of my finger-spinning tops.

Spinning tops have a surprisingly long and international history; for example, people playing with large whipping tops are pictured on Greek pottery made in about 500 BC. For more information I suggest you consult: Gould, D.W. *The Top*. Folkestone: Bailey Brothers & Swinfen, 1975.

Gould describes six patterns of top. I'll focus on just one, the finger-spinning top or what Gould calls a *twirler*. In recent times some turners have produced them with elaborate ornament and decoration. (*Ornament* is three-dimensional and on tops is often produced using a chatter tool; *decoration* is created using paint or stain.) My tops are intended to be non-precious, used rather than contemplated, and are slightly educational—as shown in figure 17.1 each top's wood is named.

16.1 MAKING THE TOPS

Denser woods are preferred because the resulting tops will spin for longer. The wood must be of even density for the resulting tops to spin truely: a top shouldn't therefore include both heartwood and sapwood because the latter is less dense when seasoned.

For four tops, a workpiece's total length should be about 170 mm. Most chucking arrangements hold 3-top workpieces which are about 130-mm-long more securely. The finished diameter of tops should be between 35 and 50 mm because babies might swallow tops with smaller diameters, and children find tops with diameters greater than 50 mm difficult to spin. How I make tops is described in figures 16.2 to 16.26.

Figure 16.2 The tools I use for top turning: *clockwise from the left*: a 1-mm-diameter twist drill held in a Jacobs chuck on a No 2 MT arbor, a gauge for 38-mm diameter ground and cut from a spanner for setting the diameter of the dovetailed chucking spigot, a roughing gouge, a 10-mm-diameter detail gouge, and a 12-mm-wide skew chisel ground down to 6-mm wide to thus produce a narrow skew with a stiff blade.

The two points of the 38-mm-diameter gauge are chamfered so that the gouge will slip gently over the workpiece's spigot as the spigot's diameter reaches 38 mm.

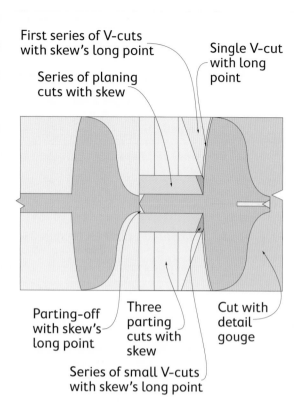

First series of V-cuts with skew's long point

Series of planing cuts with skew

Single V-cut with long point

Parting-off with skew's long point

Three parting cuts with skew

Series of small V-cuts with skew's long point

Cut with detail gouge

Figure 16.3   The series of cuts I make with the detail gouge and skew chisel to turn a top.

Figure 16.5   Using the spanner gauge and the left-hand side of my roughing gouge's cutting edge as a parting tool to cut the chucking spigot at the right-hand end of the workpiece.

Figure 16.4   Roughing a 130-mm-long workpiece to a near-cylinder with a roughing gouge.

I use the overhand grip with my left thumb on top of the gouge's blade for these cuts, and the tied-underhand grip for all other cuts.

Figure 16.6   V-cutting with the skew's long point to form a clean, flat, annular face which I'll force against the chuck jaws as the chuck is tightened. This will ensure that the workpiece is held securely and axially.

Figure 16.9   Roughing the workpiece to a true and axial cylinder using the roughing gouge presented with substantial side rake.

Figure 16.7   Cutting the spigot to a dovetail profile with the skew's short point.

Figure 16.10   Using the detail gouge to cut the right-hand end of the workpiece back to eliminate the hole left by the pin of the driving or tail center, and to start to create the desired cyma reversa profile.

Figure 16.8   About to chuck the workpiece in a four-jaw scroll chuck.

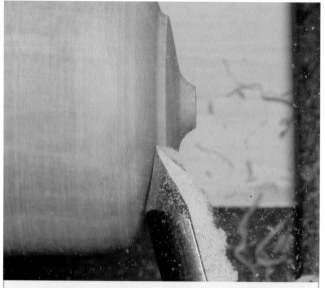

Figure 16.12   Continuing to cut the cyma-reversa profile.

Figure 16.11   Beginning to cut the cyma-reversa-profiled underside of the finger-spinning top. The cut was started by cutting horizontally to the right with the flute rotated about 30° clockwise from the vertical so that cutting was being performed by the shoulder of the cutting edge at about 45° side rake. I'm using the tied-underhand grip.

Figure 16.13   starting to axially rotate the gouge anticlockwise.

Figure 16.14 Using the skew's long point to scrape a tiny, axial, V-shaped recess in the end of the top. The diameter of the wood at the end of the workpiece is about 4 mm, 1-mm-greater than the diameter of the head of an escutcheon pin.

Figure 16.16 Scraping three ornamental V-grooves with the skew's long point.

Figure 16.15 Boring the 1-mm-diameter hole for the escutcheon pin. The Jacobs chuck holding the twist drill may be hand-held as here, or held by its Morse-taper arbor in the tailstock ram.

Figure 16.17 Starting the first deepening V-cut with the skew's long point to create the top's slightly convex top surface.

Figure 16.18   Making a clearing V-cut.

Figure 16.20   Scraping a small V-groove which acts as a guide when later writing the wood species on the top's top surface with a pyrograph.

Figure 16.19   Once the series of alternating deepening and clearing V-cuts has reached a diameter of about 15 mm, I do a slow finishing V-cut to produce a clean, slightly convex surface. I don't force the long point down further as this would crush what will be finished surface.

Figure 16.21   Making the second of a series of three parting cuts with the skew resting flat on its side on the toolrest.

Figure 16.22 Making the last of the three parting cuts.

Figure 16.24 Planing the stem from left to right.

Figure 16.23 Making a gentle V-cut to continue producing the finished surface of the top's top. Prior to this cut I made a couple of similar cuts to create space to the left so that when making this V-cut I didn't leave a crushed surface.

As shown in this and the three following figures, by using V-cuts and planing cuts from left to right and from right to left I'm able to finish-turn the top's stem.

Figure 16.25 Planing the stem from right to left.

Figure 16.27 Sanding the top with 180-grit abrasive paper.

Figure 16.26 Planing the stem from left to right. The finished stems should be 15- to 20-mm-tall and 5- to 6-mm in diameter.

Figure 16.28 Parting-off with the skew's long point. Excluding the roughing- and chucking-connected operations, a top takes about two minutes to turn, sand, and part-off.

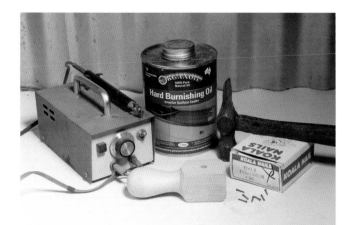

Figure 16.29 The post-turning equipment and materials I use: *left*, a hot-wire pyrograph; *front center*, an aid to hammering in escutcheon pins; *right*, the brass escutcheon pins are 12-mm-long, 1.6-mm-diameter, and have a head diameter of about 3 mm.

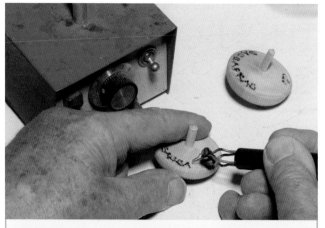

Figure 16.31 Writing the name of the wood and signing my initials with a pyrograph.

After writing on the tops, I then polish them by dunking them in an oil finish and leaving them on absorbent paper for the finish to drain and dry. It's then "Come in spinner". And remember, spinning is best achieved using the thumb and middle finger, not the thumb and index finger.

Figure 16.30 Hammering in an escutcheon pin with a cross-pein hammer. The stem of the spinning top is located in the hole in the hammering aid.

THIS BOOK'S TYPEFACES

This chapter explains how I chose the typeface families for this book, and provides an introduction to the use of digital typefaces. Such content is unknown in woodturning books, but there is a tenuous connection between woodturning and typefaces: the first printed woodturning instruction in English was the chapter the 'Art of Turning' in volume I of *Mechanick Exercises or the Doctrine of Handy-Works* printed and published in parts between 1677 and 1680 by Joseph Moxon (figure 17.1).[1] Moxon also wrote and published in 1683 and 1684 as

volume II of *Mechanick Exercises* the first manual on type and printing in any language.[2] My other excuse for this chapter is that readers of my books typically have wide interests and will, I believe, find its content useful when laying out their own communications.

17.1   TYPEFACES AND FONTS

If you use a computer you'll have some familiarity with using *typefaces*. A *typeface* is a 'range of alphanumeric characters which share an overall design'. A typeface family consists of a number of related typefaces; one is illustrated in figure 17.2.

Typefaces are often wrongly called *fonts*. The term *font* comes from the Middle French word *fonte* meaning 'casting', and refers to the casting of metal type at a type foundry. Figure 17.3 shows a type.

Moveable type was first used in China and Korea in the 13th century, but it was in Mainz, in what is now Germany, that Johannes Gutenberg in the middle of the fifteenth century invented the means to produce huge numbers of precisely dimensioned moveable metal type. Therefore until the introduction of photographic typesetting in the 1950s, *font* meant 'a set of metal type of a particular size, weight (thickness of character outlines) and style. Now that typography is computerised, a *font*

Figure 17.1   Joseph Moxon (1627–1691) pictured on the frontispiece of *Mathematics Made Easie* which was written, printed and published by Moxon in London in 1679. Moxon was a member of the Royal Society and a friend of scientists Robert Hooke, Robert Boyle, and Edmund Halley. Moxon was also Hydrographer by Appointment to His Majesty Charles II, a maker of maps and globes, a designer of typefaces, a cutter of type punches, and the author of the about a dozen books.
Sourced from Wikimedia Commons.

is the 'software used to produce screen and/or printed images in a particular typeface'.

Baselines

Cambridge light

Cambridge light italic

Cambridge light condensed italic

Cambridge light expanded

Cambridge light expanded italic

Cambridge regular

Cambridge regular italic

Cambridge regular condensed italic

Cambridge regular expanded

Cambridge expanded italic

Cambridge semibold

Cambridge semibold italic

Cambridge semibold condensed

Cambridge semibold condensed italic

Cambridge bold

Cambridge bold italic

Cambridge bold condensed

Cambridge bold condensed italic

Cambridge bold expanded

Cambridge bold expanded italic

Figure 17.2 Twenty typefaces of the Cambridge typeface family, here set 16/19.2. Thus, as explained in figure 17.4, the point size (height) of all these typefaces is 16, and the leading (the distance measured in points from the baseline of one line of type to the preceding baseline) is 19.2 points. (A DTP (desktop publishing point) is 1/72 (0.139) of an inch or 0.3528 mm).

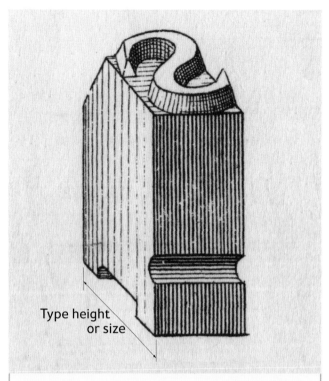

Figure 17.3 A metal type for an upper-case S. The type for a lower-case character with a descender would not have the rear chamfer because its top surface would need to extend to the type's full height to accommodate the descender's relief.

As shown in figure 17.4, the full-height flat face of a metal type from which the character relief protrudes became the basis for the bounding box for digital type.

To produce a type, a steel punch was cut. Some characters have counters. (As shown in figure 17.4, a *counter* is a 'space inside a character such as inside the bowl of a *d*'.) To produce the punch for a letter with a counter, a counterpunch was hammered into the punch before the remainder of the character was cut. The punch was then used to make a mould in which multiple copies of the type could be cast.

Scanned from the Dover edition of Diderot.[3]

17.2   USING TYPEFACES

When laying out text there are many variables. I'll discuss just five of the most important:

- the typeface family
- the size of the characters
- the vertical spacing of the lines of characters
- the horizontal spacing of the characters
- the length of the lines of characters

17.2.1   Typeface family

The advent of computers has greatly facilitated designing, distributing and using typefaces. There are now several thousand typeface families available. Those used in books are typically restrained in design, and can be separated into serif and sans-serif. (Serifs are the small, commonly but not necessarily spike-like, projections at the ends of character strokes. The word *serif* is probably derived from an Old German word for the stroke of a pen.) There are six named forms of serif. Figure 17.4 shows two: those in the top line are bracketed serifs, those projecting from the Cambridge 1 in the middle line are unbracketed slab serifs.

I used the serif font Minion Pro (top line of figure 17.4) in some earlier books, and retain it for the body text in this book. It is elegant, has a modest x height (see figure 17.5), and is nicely horizontally compact. Robert Slimbach designed it for Adobe Systems. It was released in 1990. Its name recalls that in the United States before digital typography the size of a 7-point typeface was called *minion*.

To differentiate this book's body text from the text in its illustrations and captions I decided to use a sans-serif typeface for the latter. In the earlier books in this series I used Gill Sans MT designed by Eric Gill (figure 17.6). (MT denotes that the Monotype font foundry owns the copyright for this version of Gill Sans.) I had selected Gill Sans MT because it was sufficiently different to, but didn't clash with, Minion, and both have a similar x height and a not-too-large lateral extent. However it, along with the majority of typeface families, poorly differentiates some characters.

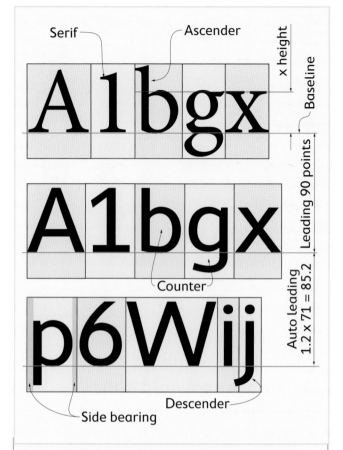

Figure 17.4   The sizing and spacing of digital typefaces. *Top line*, a serif typeface (Minion Pro regular); *middle and bottom lines*, a sans-serif typeface (Cambridge).

All the characters in this figure are of size 71 points.

The rectangles with mauve and pale-green fills are the bounding boxes for the characters. In digital typography, line spacing is measured between baselines (here colored blue), and is confusingly called *leading*.

Figure 17.5 Variation in x height for five different, regular typefaces all of size 71-point.

Figure 17.6 A self portrait by Arthur Eric Rowton Gill (1882–1940) drawn in 1927. Known as Eric Gill, he was an English sculptor, carver, engraver and typeface designer.

In 1925 Gill was commissioned by Stanley Morison, typographic advisor to the Monotype Corporation, to design the serif typeface family which came to be called *Perpetua*. In 1927 Morison saw Gill's hand-painted sans-serif lettering on a bookshop's fascia board. This lead to Morison commissioning what came to be called *Gill Sans* (used for this paragraph). Its design owes much to the typeface designed for the London Underground >

> on which Gill had earlier worked with Edward Johnston.

The biography *Eric Gill* by Fiona MacCarthy describes both Gill's many artistic achievements and his unusual propensities.[4]

Sourced from Wikimedia Commons.

17.2.2 Character differentiation

A typeface consists of upper- and lower-case letters, numerals, and glyphs (letters and numbers from other languages, and characters which aren't letters or numbers). Figure 17.7 shows several characters which are usually poorly differentiated. I first became aware of this poor differentiation while laying out the captions in Gill Sans in my 2016 accounting book *Know Accounting Graphically*. I then looked at other popular typeface families more closely, and was surprised to find that this poor differentiation is the norm in book typefaces, and especially in sans-serif typefaces.

This poor differentiation isn't usually a problem because of context. It is though for, for example, the computer passwords which you have to invent and which should to be a muddle of characters. Also where text includes calculations, poor differentiation increases the probability of confusion. I decided to search for a sans-serif typeface which avoided this probability. There were few. I chose Cambridge.

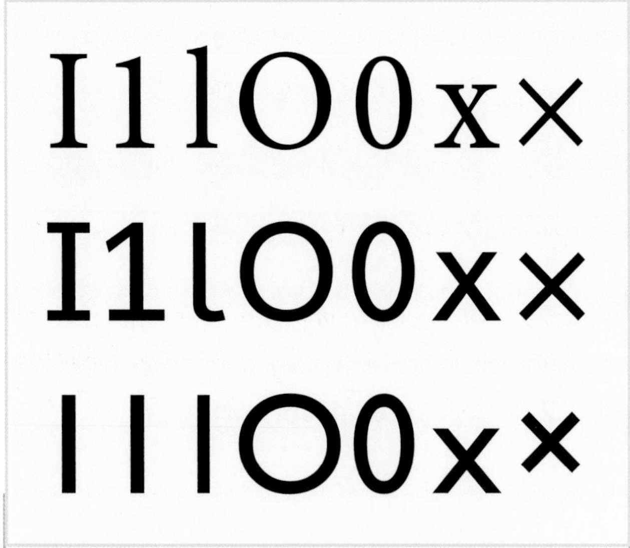

I1lOOxx

I1lOOxx

I1lOOxx

IIIOOxx

Figure 17.7 Characters which are too often poorly differentiated in typefaces are *left to right*: upper case *I*, numeral *1*, lower-case *l*, upper-case letter *O*, numeral *0*, lower case *x*, and the multiplication sign.

The regular typefaces are *top to bottom*: Minion Pro, Cambridge, and Gill Sans MT.

Cambridge is that rare typeface which clearly differentiates the problem characters, with perhaps the exception of the lower-case *x*. However, although Cambridge's slab serifs are in my opinion too big, I decided to stick with Cambridge for this book rather than create a new typeface family using software such as Fontcreator.

17.2.3 Size

Figure 17.4 illustrates that the size of a typeface is measured from just above its highest ascender to just below its lowest descender. This size is measured in points. Most readers of this book are likely to prefer a largish type size for the text. I've therefore used 11-point in both the body text and the captions. However, the same character with the same point size in different digital typefaces does not necessarily print the same height. For example, the Cambridge *A* prints a little taller than the Minion *A*. Reasons for this can be because ascender heights and descender depths can be different, as can x heights. The

relative sizes of characters can also vary; for example the Minion *A* is shorter than the Minion *b*, but the Cambridge *A* and *b* have the same height.

17.2.4 Spacing

As figure 17.3 shows, with metal type the size of a character is the height of its type measured in points. The heights of the type of all the characters in all the typefaces of the same point size are equal. To increase the vertical space between lines of metal type, strips of metal of the appropriate thickness called *leading* were locked between the lines of type. In digital typesetting the process is somewhat different.

Each character in a digital typeface is positioned within an invisible rectangle called a *bounding box*. A bounding box can be considered to have the same vertical length as its character's point size. Typically a character's bounding box will be wider than the character because of the presence of vertical bands of space to the left and right of the character called *side bearing*. (In figure 17.4 the side bearings are shown for the first character in the bottom line.) As you type characters in a horizontal line, their bounding box sides just touch. Using the process called *kerning*, you can introduce space between adjacent bounding boxes, or even overlap them.

A *baseline* is the 'imaginary horizontal line on which most of the characters in a typeset line appear to sit'. In figure 17.4 the baselines are colored blue. The vertical distance between adjacent baselines is measured in points, and is called the *leading*. The meaning of *leading* in digital typography is therefore different to its meaning in the context of metal type. All the bounding boxes for a particular size of typeface can be considered to have an internal baseline at the same distance up from the bottoms of their bounding boxes. Each character is then correctly vertically positioned relative to that baseline in its bounding box. Unless action is taking to alter the leading, it will be assumed to be Auto, that is 1.2 x the typeface's point size as figure 17.4 explains.

For 11-point type faces the Auto leading is 13.2 points. I chose the more generous leadings of 15-point for this book's body text and 14-point for its captions. The different leadings further assist in differentiating the two applications.

17.3   STYLE MANUALS

Those who wish to learn more about typefaces will find *Just My Type* a fascinating introduction.[5] *The Complete Manual of Typography* is a comprehensive treatment of its subject.[6] However the efficiency with which printed text communicates depends not only on its typography, but on how closely its layout, punctuation, etc. conform to the conventions which readers expect. These conven-

tions are explained in texts called *style manuals* (figure 17.8). Many countries have national style manuals, and there are style manuals for technical and digital publication.

17.4   ENDNOTES

1. Moxon, Joseph. *Mechanick Exercises or the Doctrine of Handy-Works*. New York: Praeger Publishers, 1970. (Originally published between 1678 and 1703.)

2. Moxon, Joseph. *Mechanick Exercises on the Whole Art of Printing*. New York: Dover Publications, 1978. (Originally published in 1683 and 1684.)

3. Diderot, Denis. *A Diderot Pictorial Encyclopedia of Trades and Industry*, volume 2. New York: Dover Publications, 1959, plate 374. (Originally published in 1752.)

4. MacCarthy, Fiona. *Eric Gill*. London: Faber and Faber, 1989.

5. Garfield, Simon. *Just My Type*. London: Profile Books, 2010.

6. Felici, James. *The Complete Manual of Typography*. Berkeley: Peachpit Press, 2003.

Figure 17.8   Style manuals from my library which aren't necessarily the most recent editions:

- *The Chicago Manual of Style*, 15th edition. Chicago: The University of Chicago Press, 2003.
- *Microsoft Manual of Style for Technical Publications Third Edition*. Richmond: Microsoft Press, 2004.
- *The Yahoo! Style Guide*. New York: St Martin's Press, 2010.
- *Merriam Webster's Standard American Style Manual*. Springfield: Merriam-Webster, 1985.
- *Style Manual*, 6th edition. John Wiley & Sons Australia, 2002.
- *The Oxford Style Manual*. Oxford: Oxford University Press, 2003.

MILLIMETERS INTO INCHES

I stated on page 11 that "for woodturners millimeters are a far more convenient unit of measurement than inches". That is particularly so for smallish turnings such as those in this book. The other advantage of the metric system is that its various units are connected by the same base as our numbering system, ten. (Twelve would, in my view, have been a better base.) However I do provide below a table of conversions for millimeters into fractions of an inch.

Millimeters	Inches	Millimeters	Inches	Millimeters	Inches	Millimeters	Inches
1	3/64	19	3/4	36	1 27/64	60	2 23/64
2	5/64	20	25/32	37	1 29/64	70	2 3/4
3	1/8	21	53/64	38	1 1/2	80	3 5/32
4	5/32	22	55/64	39	1 17/32	90	3 35/64
5	13/64	23	29/32	40	1 37/64	100	3 15/16
6	15/64	24	15/16	41	1 39/64	150	5 29/32
7	9/32	25	63/64	42	1 21/32	200	7 7/8
8	5/16	25.4	1	43	1 11/16	250	9 27/32
9	23/64	26	1 1/32	44	1 47/64	300	11 13/16
10	25/64	27	1 1/16	45	1 49/64	350	13 25/32
11	7/16	28	1 7/64	46	1 13/16	400	15 3/4
12	15/32	29	1 9/64	47	1 27/32	500	19 11/16
13	33/64	30	1 3/16	48	1 57/64	600	23 5/8
14	35/64	31	1 7/32	49	1 59/64	700	27 9/16
15	19/32	32	1 17/64	50	1 31/32	800	31 1/2
16	5/8	33	1 19/64	50.8	2	900	35 7/16
17	43/64	34	1 11/32	51	2 1/64	1,000	39 3/8
18	45/64	35	1 3/8	52	2 3/64		

INDEX